PRESIDENTIAL ACCOUNTABILITY

Presidential Accountability

New and Recurring Problems

JOHN ORMAN

CONTRIBUTIONS IN POLITICAL SCIENCE, NUMBER 254

Bernard K. Johnpoll, *Series Editor*

Greenwood Press

NEW YORK • WESTPORT, CONNECTICUT • LONDON

Library of Congress Cataloging-in-Publication Data

Orman, John M.
    Presidential accountability : New and recurring problems / John
Orman.
        p.   cm.—(Contributions in political science, ISSN 0147–1066 ;
no. 254)
    Includes bibliographical references.
    ISBN 0–313–27314–6 (lib. bdg. : alk. paper)
    1. Presidents—United States—History.   2. Executive power—United
States—History.   3. Separation of powers—United States—History.
I. Title. II. Series.
JK511.074   1990
353.03'13'09—dc20   89–26058

British Library Cataloguing in Publication Data is available.

Library of Congress Catalog Card Number: 89–26058
ISBN: 0–313–27314–6
ISSN: 0147–1066

First published in 1990

Greenwood Press, Inc.
88 Post Road West, Wesport, Connecticut   06881

Printed in the United States of America

The paper used in this book complies with the
Permanent Paper Standard issued by the National
Information Standards Organization (Z39.48–1984).

10 9 8 7 6 5 4 3 2 1

Copyright Acknowledgment

The publisher and author are grateful for permission to use the
following material:

John Orman, "Exercise of the President's Discretionary Power in
Criminal Justice Policy," *Presidential Studies Quarterly* 9, no. 4
(1979). Courtesy of *Presidential Studies Quarterly.*

For Natalie, Katie Rose, and Nicholas Demkiw-Orman,
so that they might be able to hold their presidents accountable.

Contents

Acknowledgments

I would like to thank Professors Jeff Fishel, Marjorie Hershey, John Lovell, and Maurice Baxter for helping me think about presidential accountability while I was a graduate student at Indiana University in the 1970s. My thanks also go to Thomas Cronin, Bruce Miroff, and George Edwards III, for their insights into the subject. My colleagues at Fairfield University, particularly Kevin Cassidy, Don Greenberg, and Ed Dew have been helpful in focusing in on certain aspects of abuse of presidential power.

I want especially to thank Professor Dorothy Rudoni, Ball State University, for coauthoring most of chapter 4 with me. Much of this chapter first appeared in *Presidential Studies Quarterly* 9, no. 4 (1979) and is used here by permission of R. Gordon Hoxie, editor.

I want to thank friend and Professor, Paul Hagner, Washington State University, for coauthoring sections on presidential debates with me. We first presented the section on presidential symbolic manipulation at the American Political Science Association Annual Meeting in 1977 and it is used here by permission of Paul Hagner. We both learned much about presidential accountability from the late Professor William Mullen of Washington State University.

My thanks to Sally Williams, who helped me type some sections.

I wish to thank Greenwood Press for granting me permission to use some material on presidential secrecy and deception that first appeared in my book *Presidential Secrecy and Deception: Beyond the Power to Persuade*, Greenwood Press, 1980, pp. 38–40, 46. Moreover, I wish to thank the editor of Politics and Law at Greenwood Press, Mildred Vasan, Series Editor Bernard K. Johnpoll, and Alicia S. Merritt, production editor, for helping me with this project.

Thanks go to Reenie Demkiw, Natalie, and Katie for all the good times while working on this book and while waiting for baby Nicholas.

PRESIDENTIAL
ACCOUNTABILITY

1

The Problem of Presidential Accountability

The presidency in the United States is, by many accounts, the most important political position in the world. The power of American presidents is the subject of an immense scholarly literature. The media covers the president's every move. The president is said to control "the nuclear button." He is the chief U.S. foreign policy-maker and national security manager. He is the central public policy initiator, and he is the symbol of the American state. Theoretically, he sits atop the chain of command in the American bureaucracy. He provides a check against a "misguided" Congress, and he "monopolizes public space" to use Bruce Miroff's phrase.[1] He is the most important public opinion leader in the U.S. democracy, and his control of information allows him to try to manipulate international and domestic versions of reality. For most Americans, as William Mullen has observed, the president of the United States *is* the United States government.[2]

PRESIDENTIAL POWER

The framers of the Constitution decided in 1787 that American presidential power would be separate from the judicial and the legislative branches. Not only would powers be separated, but they would be intermingled in a system of "checks and balances." The executive would be given some legislative powers like the veto, the ability to call special session, and the power to influence in the state of the union messages. The legislature had the control of the purse and the power to declare war. The House of Representatives had the power to impeach a president, and the U.S. Senate would try the indicted chief executive. The president would make war once it was officially declared, and the president had the power to pardon.

The constitutionality specified roles for the president in the vague Article II included the following:

1. Chief Executive (with no definition of what executive powers were)
2. Commander-in-Chief
3. Chief Diplomat (the president would negotiate treaties, which the Senate would have to ratify)

These roles have dramatically expanded over the 200 years since the drafting of the U.S. Constitution. The president now is also responsible for being

4. Chief of State
5. Chief Party Leader
6. Manager of Prosperity
7. Chief Opinion Leader
8. Chief Legislator or Agenda Setter, and
9. World Leader[3]

The powers of the president have expanded greatly over the years. The emergence of the United States as a great industrial nation after the Civil War gave rise to the president's mandate to help manage capitalism. The various presidential power plays and aggrandizements by powerful chief executives have added strong prerogative powers for a bold president. The advent of mass communications, like radio and television, has allowed the president to monopolize and manipulate the public space. The twentieth century saw the United States come to international power as a trade and warring partner. The expansion of the United States as a military power gave new meaning to the president's role as commander-in-chief, as the production of nuclear weapons gave the president the hitherto unknown ability to destroy the world. The rise of the welfare state gave the president unusual economic powers. The democratization of the electorate gave the president more people to represent, and the abdication of congressional responsibilities gave the president the ability to fill the vacuum of needed national leadership.

Presidential power has fluctuated from periods of "imperial presidents" to weak presidents dominated by strong legislatures. George Washington established the first precedents for presidential behavior. No one knew how a president should behave, since there had never been one. Washington provided a mix of the revolutionary war hero, celebrity, statesman, and political leader. The job description had been written with Washington in mind, but he still had to establish the early traditions. A president would not be a king, nor would he be just a figurehead.

Thomas Jefferson added the power of secret negotiations over the Louisiana Purchase, and he impounded funds. James Madison more or less defended the United States against England in 1812, and James Monroe in 1823 issued his unenforceable Monroe Doctrine. The popular Andrew Jackson moved Indians out of the Southeast and told the Supreme Court that he was not going to enforce one of their decisions. Abraham Lincoln successfully kept the Union together during the Civil War. He had to suspend the writ of habeas corpus, become a wartime commander-in-chief, and violate a few civil liberties. He issued executive orders eliminating slavery, and he was victorious. Grover Cleveland used the power of the presidency to repress labor movements, and Theodore "Teddy" Roosevelt tried to stretch American power around the world. William Taft became a key trust buster, and Woodrow Wilson showed Americans how a world war presidency would be conducted. He became virtually the director of the economy, and he suspended certain liberties like free speech and press when he sought the Espionage Act and the Sedition Acts of 1917.

Franklin D. Roosevelt took unusual steps to provide executive leadership during the depression of the 1930s. During World War II he became close to the American dictator with his broad use of domestic and foreign commander-in-chief powers. He interned Japanese-Americans in relocation centers and he set the country on the road to being a nuclear power.

Harry Truman presided over the victorious conclusion to World

War II, and he ordered two atomic bombs dropped on Japan. Truman was at the helm when the president's so-called "secret army," the Central Intelligence Agency (CIA), was set up.

Dwight Eisenhower used American presidential power to integrate the Little Rock, Arkansas, public schools by force, and he engaged in U–2 spy flights over the Soviet Union. Eisenhower overthrew Mossadegh in Iran and staged a coup in Guatemala.

John Kennedy used the CIA as his own personal tool. He tried to overthrow Fidel Castro, and his administration even engaged in assassination plots against foreign heads of state. Kennedy used nuclear blackmail to achieve his goal of getting the Soviet Union to withdraw missiles from Cuba.

Lyndon Johnson used the powers of the presidency to promote an undeclared war in Vietnam, and he engaged in CIA paramilitary war in Laos. Richard Nixon continued the presidential war in Vietnam, and he secretly ordered the bombing of Cambodia. Nixon encouraged the overthrow of Salvador Allende in Chile from 1970 to 1973, and he overstepped his bounds in the domestic arena from 1969 to 1974 with his efforts to punish his political enemies. In 1975–76 the Frank Church Committee in the Senate and the Otis Pike Committee in the House revealed a long train of presidential abuses of the intelligence communities. Presidents since F.D.R. had used the Federal Bureau of Investigation (FBI) and then the CIA for their own partisan political purposes against American dissidents. Finally, Ronald Reagan used presidential power to invade Grenada, bomb Libya, and try to overthrow Daniel Ortega and the Sandinistas in Nicaragua. Moreover, Reagan set up a secret U.S. alternative presidential government under the direction of Lt. Col. Oliver North to carry out U.S. covert policies.

Yet, despite this trend toward strong presidential leadership, the country has not had a dictator for chief executive. There are simply too many potential checks on abuse of presidential powers, including

- the House and the Senate
- the Supreme Court with decisions limiting presidential power
- American public opinion
- the opposition political party

- the American mass media
- the state and local powers
- the federal bureaucracy
- the U.S. Constitution
- the electorate
- constraining traditions and political culture

However, regardless of these checks the president has influence in the political system, and he has power. The president may try to influence other actors in the political system to do something they would not ordinarily do.

Harry Truman, and then scholar Richard Neustadt, said presidential power was "the power to persuade."[4] It is also the power to issue unilateral, nonreciprocal commands that are obeyed through reasons of loyalty, socialization, or perceptions of role and authority.

Presidents have formal and informal powers. The formal powers include those constitutionally specified as tempered by traditions, precedents, and court interpretations. Informal powers include the powers to persuade, influence, and manipulate public opinion, Congress, bureaucracy, media, parties, and national agenda.

In order to persuade, a president must use his bargaining skills. He must use his professional reputation, his personal popularity, and his ability to reason to get actors in the political system to move. A president can gain compliance through various power relationships. He might make claims that get people to respond based on

- authority
- expertise
- pragmatic calculations
- referent power
- loyalty
- affective power
- charismatic power
- guilt

The president has responsibilities in domestic policy, including economic policy, farm policy, urban, education, trade, commerce, energy, health, human services, and resources among many others. He has foreign policy responsibilities to maintain national security and to advance U.S. interests in conducting foreign relations.

Presidents also have a wide range of symbolic powers that they can use to garner support, since they can act as the symbol of the state. To most Americans, the president of the United States *is* the only true national leader.

The cycles of presidential power range from weak, do-nothing presidents to strong, so-called "imperial" presidents. In between these extremes fall most presidential administrations. A vision of the American presidency as portrayed in textbooks from World War II until the Vietnam War showed the American president as the *supreme activist* in the political system. He was the policy initiator and the one who was held accountable for all American national and international problems. He was the main agenda setter in American politics. He was all-seeing and all-knowing. He was wise and benevolent. He was heroic as he faced the "awesome" burden of the presidency. He was a strong leader.[5]

If the leader gets *too* strong, he enters the realm of the "imperial presidency." The imperial president engages in *excessive* secrecy, deception, isolation, love of trappings of office, media manipulation, unilateral warmaking, arrogance, lack of accountability, and lawlessness.[6]

On the other hand, a president may be weak and "impeded." He may not be able to lead because of the overuse of checks and balances, because of Congress and restrictions, because of the lack of statutory authority. Public opinion, media, or opinion leaders may constrain the president from certain actions. The bureaucracy may become intractable. In certain situations, the presidency may become an "impossible" job.

The president has to live up to certain myths within the political system. He is asked to be a "macho" leader.[7] He must be strong, decisive, unemotional, sports-minded, competitive, powerful, aggressive, and a "real" man. On the other hand, the president must operate in a system of contradictory expectations by citizens. He must be president of all the people, and he must be leader of his party. He must be open and honest; yet he must sometimes be closed and deceitful. He must be a democratic leader; yet he must be an innovative leader. He must be a common man who gives an extraordinary, exceptional performance in office. He must obey the law, and he must bend the rules at times.[8]

The president must strive for presidential competence and hope for presidential greatness. The competent president tries to carry out his constitutionally specified roles. He must manage domestic, economic, foreign, and national security roles. He is a persuasive president who tries to lead. He manages his staff well, and he is an efficient administrator. A "great" president, depending upon one's definition, must be an activist president who serves during a time of national crisis and who handles the crises effectively. The consensus list of great presidents includes George Washington, Thomas Jefferson, Andrew Jackson, Abraham Lincoln, Teddy Roosevelt, Woodrow Wilson, Franklin Roosevelt, and Harry Truman. Dwight Eisenhower has been upgraded to "near great."[9]

The poor presidents have been Ulysses S. Grant and Warren Harding. Andrew Johnson was impeached by the House and found innocent of charges brought against him in the Senate. Richard Nixon was impeached by a House judiciary committee for obstruction of justice, abuse of power, and contempt of Congress during the Watergate years. He resigned the presidency and then received a full, absolute pardon for all crimes he may have committed from President Gerald Ford.

In between this wide range of presidential behavior are the other twenty-six occupants of the office who range from "near great" to weak and mediocre. Presidents are rated on their abilities to manipulate other actors in the political system and to put their imprint on the institution and on history.

PRESIDENTIAL ACCOUNTABILITY

In a democracy, there must be mechanisms to hold executive power in check. The framers of the Constitution decided that the best way to hold the executive accountable so that he would not become a tyrannical king was to have a system of checks and balances, separation of powers, federalism, and a Bill of Rights. The theory was that no monarch could develop in a system that provided so many checks against runaway, unbridled, aggrandized presidential power.

The modern presidency with its emphasis on the national security state has called into question the checks that the framers left us. In celebrating the bicentennial of the Bill of Rights, it is important to examine the presidency in terms of the consequences to individual citizens and their liberty. The whole system of checks and balances, and separation of powers was tested dramatically in the 1970s during the Watergate years. Some scholars argued that the system worked and Nixon was held accountable for his actions.

Unfortunately, the lesson of what happened to Nixon never had any impact on the mechanisms of presidential accountability because Nixon's reputation was restored in the 1980s as a great statesman. He was not forced to suffer any public reprobation by the media in the 1980s over Watergate, as he made another successful comeback.

Nixon's Downfall

Former President Richard Nixon is currently trying for more political respect of sorts in the 1990s. As far as we know, he has no plans to run for office, but he is trying for some "presidential revisionism" by historians, columnists, political scientists, and citizens in order that they might rethink the Nixon years and upgrade his presidential rankings. Today as in the late 1960s, Nixon's goal is to be remembered as a great international statesman and leader. With books like *The Real War* and *The Real Peace*, Nixon hopes to offer justifications for his administration in the guise of faulty scholarship. He argues that leaders have to lie and deceive at times in order to get things done. He maintains that sometimes a great leader must break certain laws to achieve the greater good for the nation. He freely gives advice on how to be a great president and statesman. His primer on leadership and greatness would make Machiavelli proud to see that someone still took him seriously.

Nixon's hopes for a presidential upgrading (much like the one Harry Truman magically received in the mid–1970s because people wrongly started to argue that at least Truman told the truth) rest on the assumption that the attention span of the American people is one week and their sense of history deals with what happened in the last two weeks. Nixon is hoping that many people will argue that he was a great president who might have done some illegal things, but so do all other presidents. Nixon just got caught.

Nixon did much more than just get caught. One might be able to go back and find questionable uses of presidential power by Lincoln, Wilson, and both Roosevelts, and one might be able to point to the deception of Kennedy and Johnson with respect to the Indochina war. One might bring up Harding and the Teapot Dome scandals. Yet Nixon's central problem was the scope and magnitude of his presidential corruption. In almost every category of presidential corruption that a scholar might develop, Nixon participated, and he leads in most categories.

Before one utters the words one more time that Nixon just got caught, one should remember the following:

1. He was an unindicted coconspirator in the eyes of the Watergate grand jury.
2. He secretly bombed a neutral country for some fourteen months without informing Congress or the people.
3. Nixon and Henry Kissinger plotted to assassinate General Rene Schneider of Chile because the general did not believe in military coups against democratically elected leaders like Salvador Allende.
4. Nixon used taxpayers' money for his own private concerns to improve properties at San Clemente and Key Biscayne.
5. Nixon and Henry Kissinger tried to make it impossible for Allende to govern.
6. Nixon used the Internal Revenue Service to audit returns of his political enemies to harass them.
7. Nixon had his own White House secret police called "the Plumbers."
8. Nixon tried to wiretap and bug the Democratic National Headquarters.
9. Nixon tried to break into Daniel Ellsberg's psychiatrist's office to get "dirt" on the man who leaked the *Pentagon Papers*.
10. He evaded paying his fair share of income tax while he was president because his accountant illegally backdated a transaction.
11. He lied about his involvement in the Watergate coverup.
12. He destroyed evidence in a criminal trial.
13. He talked about raising hush money to keep defendants quiet.

14. He counseled witnesses to remain silent or to say "I do not recall" when asked about Watergate matters.

15. He used unethical and illegal campaign tactics in the 1972 election. He accepted illegal campaign contributions from large corporations.

16. He secretly bombed Laos for one year.

17. He used the FBI for domestic surveillance and harassment against law-abiding citizens who opposed his policies.

18. He used the CIA to get his political enemies.

19. He wiretapped journalists.

20. Nixon was indicted and impeached by the House Judiciary Committee for obstruction of justice, abuse of power, and contempt of Congress, but he resigned before the full House of Representatives could impeach him. Then he received a full, unconditional, absolute pardon from appointed President Gerald Ford.

In all of this it was clear that it was something about Nixon's personality that pushed him to extremes. Other presidents may have done some of these things, but Nixon had done it all.

THE PROBLEM OF PRESIDENTIAL BEHAVIOR

Shocked by the outrageous presidential misbehavior of Watergate, Congress made efforts to reassert itself in executive oversight and to regain a partnership with the president in foreign policy during the 1970s. Nevertheless, the institutionalization of presidential accountability did not become sufficiently well established to check the excesses of the Reagan administration. Ronald Reagan's covert wars in Central America, his bombing of Libya, and his handling of the Iran-Contra scandal all gave witness to the return of imperial presidency to American politics less than a decade after Watergate had supposedly ended the runaway presidency. The political system always conducts the debate over whether presidents have too much or too little power. Scholars argue over the value of strong presidents versus weak presidents. Yet the problem of how to keep strong presidents in line with democratic principles has never been resolved.

The president's behavior in our political system has become so mythologized that an understanding of it has been blocked. There are still problems that strain the fragile mechanisms of accountability in the United States. The problems of executives who would take manipulative actions in secretive and deceptive fashion remain in the national security arena. The problem of who shall define a state secret remains with the political system as does a possibility of intelligence abuses by the CIA and FBI. The danger of the extremely popular "active-positive" president is still a challenge to democracy. Though Barber clearly pointed out the problems for the political system of "active-negatives," he overlooked the dangers of "active-positives."[10] The behavior of the popular president Ronald Reagan in the 1980s suggests that nice guys can cause many problems for democratic accountability.

The message of Irangate under the Reagan administration is that we need to return to thinking about problems of presidential accountability. Reagan's secrecy and deception in Irangate was in many ways more troublesome than the excesses of Watergate. Reagan tried to establish a secret government that was accountable to no one.

One need not focus on personality deficiencies of various presidents to explain presidential behavior. One can look at the institutional chances that the accumulation of powers, the isolation, the secrecy system, and the presidential myth afford for the incumbent to engage in certain behavior.

When the framers wrote the United States Constitution, the American president was to help in establishing justice, ensuring domestic tranquility, promoting the general welfare, providing for the common defense, and in securing the blessings of liberty. Sadly in almost two hundred years of presidential efforts to achieve these five values, the U.S. president seems capable in only two of the five key values of the American constitutional experience. American presidents have done a satisfactory job in providing for the common defense and ensuring domestic tranquility. Yet in pursuing these two values the American president has often crossed the line into a counterproductive pursuit. A preoccupation with the common defense can lead to warmongering, and a commitment to domestic tranquility can lead to repression. Unfortunately, this has been the case too often in American presidential politics.

The American presidency has often failed in the three other values that the president was ordered to pursue: justice, general welfare, and liberty. When domestic clashes and constitutional crises come to shove in American presidential politics, more often than not, the American president has been on the side of the oppressor rather than the oppressed; on the side of capital rather than labor; on the side of injustice rather than fairness; and on the side of anti-libertarians rather than democrats.

American presidents have acted to preserve the status quo, and they have acted as "the guardian of the system."[11] Presidents became the capitalists' "captain," and they became corporate cheerleaders. When Calvin Coolidge stated that the business of America was business, he was making a statement that might just as well have been credited to an earlier president like George Washington. Edward Greenberg observed, "As capitalism came to require an activist, interventionist government to support, coordinate, protect, subsidize, and sustain its main economic institutions and processes, so too did this new form of government require a steady hand at the helm ... this steady hand could only be that of the president."[12]

American presidents have done their best to defend corporate capitalism whether it involves fighting abroad, increasing the military-industrial complex, or engaging in tactics to quell dissenters of the capitalist-corporate system. Presidents have tried imperialist wars, civil wars, secret wars, world wars, guerrilla wars, "police actions," and even atomic wars to defend the system. They have pursued policies designed to "fight for peace" and to build up American "defenses." They have struggled to keep militant protestors from changing the political system.

The framers of the Constitution still intended that the president would be accountable to the electorate as a whole. This research will survey the current state of affairs in keeping the president accountable in the aftermath of the Reagan administration. The study will look at five major areas of concern for students of the presidency who want to check presidential power that oversteps the limits of the U.S. Constitution. Those problem areas concern: (1) presidents, national security, and civil liberties; (2) controlling the intelligence community; (3) the politicized nature of the Justice Department; (4) celebrity politics and symbolic manipulation; and (5) the popularity of the Reagan administration and implications for accountability.

Chapter 2 investigates the checkered past of American presidents with respect to protecting civil liberties. Especially in the climate of the national security state, American presidents have not provided a model of leadership in protecting civil liberties and civil rights. Chapter 3 examines the problems for presidential accountability posed by the intelligence community. Chapter 4 looks at the exercise of the president's discretionary power in the criminal justice policy arena. This area causes alarm for students of presidential accountability because of the nature of politicized justice. In chapter 5 the newer phenomenon of "celebrity politics" is explored in terms of the consequences for citizens who want to keep the American president in check. In chapter 6, the lessons of the popular Reagan presidency on presidential accountability are outlined. Finally, chapter 7 concludes by lamenting the loss of presidential accountability in the American political system. The ascension of George Bush to the presidency represented the triumph of forces that are antithetical to presidential accountability. Bush, director of the Central Intelligence Agency in the 1970s, never had to account for his role in covert operations that ran wild while he was vice president in 1981–89. It is highly unlikely that he will be asked to account for his actions in the arms-for-hostages trading with Iran, the covert war in Nicaragua, the resupplying of the Contras, and the Oliver North–William Casey secret network of extraconstitutional covert operations. Given that Bush was not called upon to account for these actions, one wonders what this bodes for the future of American democracy in the 1990s. Bush may get the impression that he can continue to engage in these unilateral covert operations without the fear of public reprobation or media scrutiny. He may well be correct if that is his position.

NOTES

1. Bruce Miroff, "Monopolizing the Public Space: The President as a Problem for Democratic Politics," in *Rethinking the Presidency*, ed. Thomas E. Cronin (Boston: Little, Brown, 1982), pp. 218–232.

2. William Mullen, *Presidential Power and Politics* (New York: St. Martin's, 1976), p. 1.

3. Clinton Rossiter, *The American Presidency*, rev. ed. (New York: Harcourt Brace Jovanovich, 1960), pp. 13–40.

4. Richard Neustadt, *Presidential Power*, 2d ed. (New York: John Wiley and Sons, 1976), pp. 77, 78.

5. Thomas Cronin, *The State of the Presidency*, 2d ed. (Boston: Little, Brown 1980), p. 84.

6. Arthur Schlesinger, Jr., *The Imperial Presidency* (Boston: Houghton Mifflin, 1973), pp. 9–12.

7. John Orman, *Comparing Presidential Behavior: Carter, Reagan and the Macho Presidential Style* (Westport, Conn.: Greenwood Press, 1987), pp. 7–8.

8. Cronin, *The State of the Presidency*, pp. 3–22.

9. The Schlesinger polls on presidential greatness, Arthur Schlesinger, Sr., "The U.S. Presidents," *Life*, November 1, 1948, p. 65, and Schlesinger, "Our Presidents: A Rating by 75 Historians," *The New York Times Magazine*, July 29, 1962, pp. 12ff.

10. James Barber, *The Presidential Character*, 2d ed. (Englewood Cliffs, N.J.: Prentice-Hall, 1977), pp. 11–14.

11. For "guardian of the system" analysis see Michael Parenti, *Democracy for the Few*, 4th ed. (New York: St. Martin's, 1983), pp. 261–282.

12. Edward Greenberg, *The American Political System: A Radical Approach*, 3d ed. (Boston: Little, Brown, 1983), pp. 236–268.

2

Presidents, National Security, and Civil Liberties

Before Watergate and the CIA/FBI revelations in the 1970s, the advocates of the strong presidency did not view the president of the United States as a threat to individual civil liberty. Indeed, one proponent of strong presidential power, James M. Burns, argued that the president was the guardian of individual liberty. Writing as late as 1973, he noted:

The powerful modern Presidency has in fact become the most effective single protector of individual liberty in our governmental system. To heighten the paradox, recent Presidents who had the very means of oppression that the republicans feared—a huge centralized military establishment and a far-flung federal law enforcement agency—have protected civil liberty far more than they have restricted it.[1]

Even without the CIA/FBI revelations of the 1970s, Burns's argument was suspect, given the mixed record of the history of presidential support for the Bill of Rights.

The mixed record of presidential support for civil liberties dates at least to John Adams and his support for the Alien and Sedition Acts in 1798. The Sedition Act indicated an inability on Adams's part to take criticism during a "national security" crisis, as the act considered it a high misdemeanor for any person to conspire to oppose or to impede any measures, operations, or laws of the United States. For anyone to write, publish, or print "any false, scandalous and malicious writing...against the government of the United States or either house of the Congress..., or the President..., with the intent to defame..., or to bring them or either of them, into contempt or disrepute; or to excite against them, or either or any of them, the hatred of the good people of the United States was a crime."[2]

Thomas Jefferson, who had secretly opposed the Alien and Sedition Acts during the original hysteria, even argued when he was president that the states should regulate the press. Jefferson sought a "few wholesome prosecutions" from the states during his administration's battle with the press, and Jefferson hardly protected civil liberties in the handling of the Aaron Burr conspiracy case.[3] Andrew Jackson responded in a novel way to his internal security "threat" by pushing through Congress the Indian Removal Act, which gave the president powers to relocate all Indian tribes to the west of the Mississippi River.[4] Moreover, Jackson asked his postmaster general to stop the distribution of abolitionist literature in the South.[5]

During the Civil War Abraham Lincoln suspended the writ of habeas corpus and ordered civilians to be tried in military tribunals in some areas of the country. Theodore Roosevelt, in response to the assassination of William McKinley in 1901, became the leading actor in the Anarchist Scare of 1901–1903. The scare culminated in the passage of a law by Congress in 1903 that penalized persons solely on the basis of views, group affiliations, and advocacy rather than the commission of a crime.[6]

Woodrow Wilson's handling of antiwar dissent during World War I is no milestone in the defense of civil liberties. In fact, Wilson set more precedents for squelching dissenters than Lincoln used in the Civil War. Modern presidents then came to believe that during wartime it was acceptable to curb such liberties. Wilson's efforts to punish Eugene Debs and Alice Paul stand out as his quintessential examples of presidential repression.

WILSON VERSUS DEBS

Rarely does a person from the militant, radical, progressive side of American politics achieve national popularity, but Eugene Debs managed to do so. For a period of twenty-six years from 1894 to 1920, Gene Debs made headlines by saying no to capitalist presidents from Grover Cleveland to Woodrow Wilson. He was America's quintessential militant labor leader, socialist, and antiwar speaker during this period. He gave American presidents strong challenges, and his organizational abilities threatened the status quo. American presidents moved to quiet Debs's opposition on numerous occasions.

In June 1894 the workers at the Pullman Car Company protested their poor wages, long hours, and horrible living conditions by going on strike. Negotiations between the workers and the Pullman company broke down, and the workers felt that they had only one option left, to withhold their labor. The national American Railway Union (ARU) was holding its convention in Chicago at the time of the Pullman strike, and the Pullman workers asked Debs and the union for support. Debs persuaded the convention to support the workers in new negotiations with the Pullman Car Company. The Pullman officials refused to negotiate once again, and Debs called for American Railway Union support for the Pullman workers in the form of ARU members refusing to work on any trains that included Pullman cars. Debs's involvement quickly led many opinion leaders to call the action "Debs's Rebellion."

Debs became the central focus of the strike for authorities. He worked all of his waking hours to help coordinate the strike. The railroads refused to drop Pullman cars and appealed to the state government for help. Illinois Governor John Altgeld refused to move against Debs and the workers, since he believed that they had legitimate claims against the Pullman Company. The federal government was more forthcoming with repressive actions. Grover Cleveland's attorney general Richard Olney got the courts to issue a federal injunction, which ordered an end to the strike. Then President Cleveland sent in federal troops, scabs, hired strikebreakers, and marshals to enforce the federal order.

Debs and the workers decided to ignore the federal injunction by claiming that workers had a right to withhold their labor. The Pullman strike then turned violent as workers and federal troops clashed. The federal court moved quickly to indict Debs for contempt of court, and he was charged with conspiracy. The conspiracy trial was never completed because of a juror's illness, but Debs was still sentenced to one half year in Woodstock Jail for contempt of court. With their leader in jail and with federal troops fighting them at every level, the workers for the American Railway Union finally had to give in. The Pullman strike failed, and the American Railway Union began to fade as fast as it had grown.

The crucial interaction in the strike was the confrontation between President Grover Cleveland and Gene Debs. Cleveland scored high marks from capitalists, conservatives, and presidential watchers for his decisive use of federal police power to put down a rebellion. The press viewed Debs as a militant protestor who deserved whatever Cleveland decided to give him.

The Pullman Strike and President Cleveland's response to it became the event that radicalized Debs. While serving his sentence in the Woodstock Jail, he started reading socialist political thought, and by the time of his release, he began to talk about the socialist solution to help working people in the fight against capitalists. He founded the Socialist party of America and in 1900 ran for president of the United States, receiving about 96,000 votes. In 1904 Debs raised his rhetoric and concerns for working people once again to the agenda of presidential politics by running for president and getting about 400,000 votes. He continued his brand of social movement politics in the presidential arena by running for president in 1908 and in 1912. He was a great orator, and he drew large crowds all over America as he campaigned. In 1916 Debs tried to run for Congress from Terre Haute, and he was once again defeated.

By 1918 Debs was having a major confrontation once again with another American president. This time Debs and Woodrow Wilson clashed over Debs's strong antiwar views. On June 16, 1918, Debs gave his famous antiwar speech in Canton, Ohio. Debs's troubles with the Wilson administration stemmed from his rhetoric in the Canton speech. Debs told the audience:

The Master class has always declared the wars; the subject class has always fought the battles. The master class has had all to gain and nothing to lose; while the subject class has had nothing to gain and all to lose—especially their lives.[7]

Debs knew the contents of his speech would violate the harsh Espionage and Alien and Sedition Acts of 1917, but he was not afraid of the consequences. He said,

They may put those boys in jail and some of the rest of us in jail, but they cannot jail the whole Socialist movement. Those prison bars may separate their bodies from us, but their souls are here this afternoon. They are simply paying the penalty that all men have paid in all the ages of history for standing erect and seeking to pave the way for better conditions for mankind.[8]

After his speech Debs was arrested and charged with violating the Espionage Act. He was released on bail in Cleveland and returned to his native Terre Haute, Indiana, to prepare his defense. His pending trial meant much to the great orator. As one reporter noted:

He spoke of it in his quiet way as his simple opportunity to serve the cause. He said that he had always felt like a member of the rank and file, and now he had his chance to travel along the road the ordinary man had to follow.... He was an old man, broken in health, facing, without flinching, without budging an eyelid, a possibility of twenty years in jail.[9]

Gene Debs had always been a romantic figure for the left in the United States. He was to rise to even larger mythical status for the left during his momentous trial.

Serving as his own attorney, Debs spoke to the jury when he had his chance. Even though Debs thought he could make his free speech case to the jury of citizens in Cleveland, he underestimated how much the jury was stacked against him. Ray Ginger tells how the jury was selected:

The jury... had a predisposition against the defendant. Jury panels in the Federal District Court of Cleveland were not chosen at random from the list of property holders of voters. The method used was far more selective. County Judges from the Federal District recommended to the Clerk of the District Court those men in their counties whom they would consider qualified for jury duty. The jury was then chosen from this panel. Thus the entire venire of one hundred men, from which Debs' jury was chosen, had an average age of seventy years, and came from the wealthy and respectable class of citizens.[10]

Moreover, the local press raged on against the likes of Gene Debs. The *Cleveland Press* reported to its readers:

Debs is doing more to aid the Hun Kaiser than all the pro-German Germans in America. He is of greater assistance to the Boches in France than are the Turks, Bulgarians, and Austrians. His Canton speech, even now being spread through all Germany and German trenches, will kill more American soldiers than all German submarines that hunt American transport ships.[11]

Even in such a harsh environment, Debs believed that he could take on the Wilson administration and win a victory for free speech at his trial. Debs told the jury that he was not guilty of any part of the indictment and that he felt he had a right to speak out against the war. He then soared off into the land of the socialist martyr, maintaining,

I would rather a thousand times be a free soul in jail than to be a sycophant and coward in the streets. They put those boys in jail . . . but they cannot put the whole Socialist movement in jail. . . . If there had not been men and women in the past who had the moral courage to go to jail, we would still be in the jungles.[12]

Debs did address the constitutionality of the Espionage Act passed by a supportive Congress to stifle critics of Wilson's war efforts. Debs argued,

I believe in the right of free speech, in war as well as in peace. I would not under any circumstances gag the lips of my bitterest enemy. I would under no circumstances suppress free speech. . . . I have told you that I am no lawyer, but it seems to me that I know enough to know that if Congress enacts any law that conflicts with any provision in the Constitution, that law is void. If the Espionage Law finally stands, then the Constitution of the United States is dead.[13]

He concluded his famous speech to the jury by framing the consequences of their decision. He boldly proclaimed:

I am the smallest part of the trial. I have lived long enough to realize my own personal insignificance in relation to a great issue that involves the welfare of the whole people. . . . There is an infinitely greater issue that is being tried today in this court, though you may not be conscious of it. American institutions are on trial here before American citizens. The future will render the final verdict.[14]

Debs had his moment in the rhetorical sunlight, and the jury convicted him of the charges brought against him by the Wilson government. He hoped to appeal the verdict to the Supreme Court, but the Court ruled against him. When Debs received the Supreme Court verdict at his home in Terre Haute, he told reporters:

The decision is perfectly consistent with the character of the Supreme Court as a ruling class tribunal.... Great issues are not decided by the courts but by the people. I stand by every word of the Canton Speech. I despise the Espionage Law with every drop of blood in my veins, and I defy the Supreme Court and all the powers of capitalism to do their worst.[15]

Debs was sentenced to ten years in prison for his speech, and he was disenfranchised for life. In 1920 he ran for the presidency for the last time, this time from a federal prison in Atlanta, Georgia. His speeches against the Democrats and the Wilson administration were censored by Wilson supporters before they could be released from the prison. Nevertheless, Debs garnered about 1 million votes while running from prison. Wilson had a personal hatred for Gene Debs and refused to pardon him when he left office. The new Republican president, Warren Harding, finally commuted Debs's sentence to time served and released him from prison on Christmas Day, 1921. The tired and beaten socialist returned to Terre Haute, Indiana, where he lived until 1926.

Debs provided a model for militants and social movements in their efforts to take on American presidents and the American political system. Though Debs was often defeated by presidential repression, his charismatic personality and his unusual oratorical skills allowed him to reach a large following. Within a decade after his death, most of the reforms that Debs fought to achieve for working people were enacted into law.

WILSON VERSUS ALICE PAUL

The saga of Alice Paul is a political biography of one of the most important political activists in the twentieth century. Alice Paul's single-minded pursuit of social justice for women is a story of remarkable persistence and tenacity. Paul provided a shining example for all social activists and citizens who struggle for social justice.

For mass-movement politics, Alice Paul used innovative tactics like mass marches on Washington, D.C., picketing the White House, nonviolent civil disobedience, and hunger strikes. Her leadership provided the militant model for other social movements to come in the twentieth century. In congressional politics, Alice Paul provided textbook examples of how to lobby an American president and Congress to get your particular legislation passed when she worked for proposal of the suffrage amendment to the United States Constitution. In grass-roots politics, she showed how to organize effectively and how to lead a social movement. In state politics, Alice Paul provided lessons on how to mobilize efforts on state capitals to achieve ratification of the Nineteenth Amendment. In political theory and legal philosophy, Paul provided the momentum for her proposed equal rights amendment, which would provide equality under the law regardless of one's sex. Finally, with respect to international politics, Alice Paul became an international feminist and a well-known peace activist. Her life exemplifies the history of the women's movement in the United States.

In the fall of 1907 Alice Paul went to Woodbrook, England, to study at a Quaker school called Woodbrook Settlement for Social Work, and she also took courses at the University of Birmingham. At the university Alice Paul attended a guest lecture by Christabel Pankhurst, who was the daughter of the famous suffrage militant in England, Emmeline Pankhurst. Alice Paul had never heard of her before, but she was shocked when the men in the audience yelled and shouted during her speech to drown out her every word. From that moment, Alice Paul became very excited about working for the English suffrage movement.[16]

In England, Paul joined the Women's Social and Political Union, which was led by the Pankhursts. She also attended the London School of Economics while in England, but in 1909 just as she was preparing to return to the United States, she started devoting more time to the movement and less to studies. Just before she was to sail home, she was arrested for marching on Parliament with other members of the Women's Social and Political Union. She had to postpone her trip because she had to stay in the country for her trial. Before she left England, she was to be arrested seven times and jailed three times. In July and September 1909 she went on hunger strikes to win her release from prison.[17]

Alice Paul's last arrest in England became a news story in the United States. *The New York Times* reported on November 10 that the Lord Mayor's feast and inauguration in London was disrupted by militant feminists who threw stones through a stained glass window.[18] The paper indicated that two women had been arrested but gave no names. The next day, the *Times* published the name of Alice Paul as one of the women who threw the stones. The account said her mother was "much agitated when she learned of her daughter's predicament" and that her mother knew her daughter was in the suffrage movement but "did not know that she had gone so far." Moreover, the paper reported, her friends in Philadelphia were "much surprised that she should suddenly have become so militant."[19]

Alice Paul was sentenced to one month of hard labor at the Holloway Jail. She went on a hunger strike and was force-fed by the authorities. She described the experience:

They tied us down with bonds around our legs, chests, and necks. Then the doctors and warders held us down and forced a tube five or six feet long, about the size of a finger, through the nostrils to the stomach. . . . It always caused my nose to bleed and brought out a perspiration all over me. I had fits of trembling, and I never went through the experience without weeping and sometimes crying aloud.[20]

When she returned to the United States, Alice Paul had become well schooled in the tactics of the militant English suffrage movement. *The New York Times* told readers that she "Won't Try to Start Suffrage War Here."[21] In fact, Alice Paul was ready to take up the task and to start organizing a militant branch of the United States suffrage movement.

Woodrow Wilson became the first U.S. president to use his office to secure and promote the woman's suffrage amendment, but he came to this position after a long period of education by militant feminists like Alice Paul and moderates like Carrie Chapman Catt. Clearly without the lobbying effort led by Alice Paul and the National Women's Party, the national constitutional amendment would not have reached the agenda of public controversy. Moreover, without Alice Paul's efforts to secure support of the president for her position, the Nineteenth Amendment to the U.S. Constitution would not have been successfully proposed.

During the campaign of 1912, Wilson refused to support woman's suffrage. Wilson used to like to say on the campaign trail that he approved of women's participation in politics, but he would not support the constitutional amendment for the right to vote. During one campaign stop a New York feminist Maude Malone interrupted Wilson in the middle of his speech and asked him to state his position clearly on women's rights. Wilson refused to discuss the subject and continued his speech. Malone kept interrupting Wilson until finally a guard removed the feminist.[22] Wilson had told reporters that suffrage was a state, not a national, issue, and thus he did not intend to be questioned about his views.[23]

Alice Paul decided that Wilson needed to be educated on the issue, using methods she had learned from the radical feminists Emmeline, Christabel, and Sylvia Pankhurst in England. On the eve of Wilson's inauguration, Alice Paul planned a huge demonstration in Washington, D.C., of some 8,000 demonstrators to protest the fact that women did not have suffrage. Onlookers became enraged at the protest, and some attacked the marchers as police failed to provide protection. This riot situation took much of the national attention away from Wilson's inauguration and was the beginning of the focused efforts to get the president to support the national amendment actively.

In 1913 Alice Paul organized three meetings with Woodrow Wilson to discuss the possibility of the president's support for the national amendment. After the meetings Wilson still refused to place this amendment at the top of his legislative priorities. By the end of the fifth meeting Wilson had indicated that since his political party had taken no position on the amendment, he could not take the lead as president of the United States to force it onto the national agenda.[24]

In 1914 Paul turned her attention to the congressional elections and the idea of electoral accountability. She argued that since Democrats were the party in power and since they failed to act on the amendment, then feminists should actively campaign against the Democratic party. Wilson was not impressed with such logic. However, he did meet with three delegations of feminists in 1914 and again in 1915 to discuss the amendment. Each time he told them it was a states' rights problem.[25]

When Wilson had a chance to vote for woman's suffrage in his state of New Jersey referendum in October 1915, he told reporters that he would vote for suffrage within New Jersey but that it was still a matter for each state to decide. He did not feel it was a presidential, congressional, or party question.

However, it had become a presidential, congressional and party question. In 1914 the U.S. Senate finally took a vote on the so-called Susan B. Anthony Amendment. For the first time, the amendment received majority support 35 to 34 but it did not receive the required two-thirds majority needed for passage. The measure was reintroduced within one day of its defeat, and the lobbying process started over again.

Alice Paul's group continued to lobby the president. In one exchange, Rheta Dorr scored impressive points against Wilson's arguments with the help of Anna Kelton Wiley:

Wiley: Granted that it is a state matter, would it not give this great movement an impetus if the Resolution now pending before Congress passed?

Wilson: But the Resolution is an Amendment to the Constitution.

Wiley: The States would have to pass upon it before it became an Amendment, would it not be a State matter then?

Wilson: Yes, but by a very different process, for by that process it would be forced upon the minority; they would have to accept it.

Dorr: They could reject it if they wished to. Three-fourths of the States would have to pass it.

Wilson: Yes, but the other fourth could not reject it.

Dorr: Mr. President, don't you think that when the Constitution was framed it was agreed that when three-fourths of the States wanted a reform, the other fourth should accept it also?

Wilson: I cannot say what was agreed upon. I can only say that I have tried to answer your question, and I do not think it is quite proper that I submit myself to cross-examination.

Dorr: Very well, we will not cross-examine you further.[26]

In 1915 the issue had come to the national agenda of the House of Representatives and was defeated by 174 yes to 204 no votes. Alice Paul and the Woman's party then turned their attention to the 1916 national elections and the political parties. The Democrats included a women's suffrage plank in their party platform, but it was worded to be read as a states' rights issue. Paul and Carrie Catt were more successful with the out party, since the Republicans' presidential candidate Charles Hughes went beyond his party platform, which supported woman's suffrage from a states' rights perspective to endorse the Susan B. Anthony Constitutional Amendment. Wilson could not be persuaded that he should also go beyond his party platform to support the amendment. The stands of both candidates were very significant, however, since both presidential candidates supported the right of women to vote.

After the 1916 election, which Wilson just barely won in the electoral college, feminists tried to impress Wilson with the fact that a majority of women who could vote in 1916 supported him for his peace candidacy. They argued that in such a close election, Wilson owed his success to female support. In early January 1917 Wilson could not be moved to support the constitutional amendment for women's suffrage, so that Alice Paul and the Woman's party started new, more militant tactics, such as daily picketing in front of the White House along with the usual parades and demonstrations.

The picketing against the president added a dramatic confrontation that the news media quickly picked up and reported. The pickets worked daily, except for Sunday, from January 10, 1917, until the April 6, 1917, declaration of war on Germany, without much interference from authorities. Mass demonstrations were organized to coincide with Wilson's second inauguration as Alice Paul kept up the pressure.

Once the United States entered in the war, the daily pickets became an embarrassment for the Wilson administration. The pickets criticized Wilson for fighting a war to make the world "safe for democracy" when the United States did not allow over half of its citizens (women) to participate under the national constitution. The picket carriers were often attacked by citizens and denounced by newspaper editorials for continuing their protests while the war was going on. Alice Paul responded by noting that if picketing the White House was legal before the war, then it was legal during the war. As one feminist noted, "I have no son to give to my country to fight for democracy abroad and so I send my daughter to Washington to fight for democracy at home."[27]

Indeed, it was a fight. Picketing after the United States entered the war became very risky business. Some days the District of Columbia police would arrest pickets for blocking access to the White House, and on other days the police would arrest pickets for blocking traffic on the streets. Some days the police would watch as the pickets did their daily duty and would encourage them with friendly gestures. Picketers never knew when orders from higher authorities would come down to "clear the streets." Wilson was clearly embarrassed by the feminist attacks on his lack of commitment to democracy at home. Yet he always tried to make it clear to reporters that he would not be influenced by demonstrators in the streets. Wilson even wrote to Carrie Chapman Catt during the campaign for New York State suffrage to say that he hoped the pickets had not hurt her cause in New York. Wilson wrote on October 13, 1917:

My Dear Mrs. Catt:
   May I not express to you my very deep interest in the campaign in New York for the adoption of Woman Suffrage, and may I not say that I hope that no voter will be influenced in his decision with regard to this matter by anything which the so-called pickets may have done here in Washington? However justly they may have laid themselves open to serious criticism, their action represents, I am sure, so small a fraction of the women of the country who are urging the adoption of Woman Suffrage that it would be most unfair and argue a narrow view to allow their actions to prejudice the cause itself. I am very anxious to see the great State of New York set a great example in this matter.
                                        Cordially and Sincerely,
                                        WOODROW WILSON[28]

   At the center of media publicity was the treatment of Alice Paul by authorities. She was arrested with other picketing women in October 1917. She carried a banner saying in Woodrow Wilson's words, "The Time Has Come to Conquer or Submit. For Us There Can Be But One Choice. We Have Made It." She was sentenced to seven months in jail for this expression. When word surfaced that she had gone to jail, more and more women showed up to give their support to the suffrage movement.

In the Occoquan Workhouse a picketer was held in effect as a political prisoner. Moreover, Paul was separated from other feminists when the authorities put her in St. Elizabeth's Insane Asylum. She went on a hunger strike and demanded better treatment for the other female protestors who had been arrested. After going for seventy-eight hours without food, the hospital authorities force-fed her.

Alice Paul's sister Helen came to Washington to protest the treatment of Alice. She said:

I told Mr. Zinkham that he would kill my sister if he forcibly fed her. She has never been able to tell me about her experience in England, it was so horrible, and I know she cannot go through with it again. How can such a brutal thing be thought of when all she is asking is decent treatment for the others imprisoned with her? . . . I know she has bitterly opposed the Democratic Party, but I cannot believe that the President or the men he has appointed will deliberately risk her life in this way.[29]

A delegation of women marched on the government psychopathic hospital to protest treatment of Alice Paul, and she yelled out the window, "Many of you will probably be here tomorrow, I want to say to you now that you will find conditions intolerable. You must make it clear from the first that you are political offenders and demand that you be treated as such."[30] When asked by a picketer how she felt, Alice Paul said:

Oh, I am all right. I am being forcibly fed three times a day. It is worse than in England. There they feed you only twice. I am able to prevent them from giving me half of what they bring, but I have not the strength to prevent them from forcing me to take some.[31]

Alice Paul hated force-feeding; yet, she endured the brutal measure in the psychopathic ward along with fellow hunger striker Rose Winslow. Dudley Malone, personal counsel for Alice Paul, denounced the government's behavior to the press. He said:

I was shocked to find that Miss Paul, because she is the leader of the National Woman's Party, had been singled out from among the other suffragists and transferred to the psychopathic ward, in spite of her demand to see her personal physician and her attorney. Miss Paul is imprisoned in a room in the midst of insane patients, whose shrieks she can hear day and night.... I talked with Miss Paul... and she is more sane than any of the administration officials who have been responsible for this outrage.[32]

After Malone and the National Woman's party publicized the treatment Alice Paul was receiving, she was released from the psychopathic ward and taken to the hospital section. Finally, on November 27, the judge who had sentenced Alice Paul and the other hunger strikers to jail ordered their release.

Through these militant activities, Alice Paul had an impact on policy. Wilson had been convinced that women should be allowed to vote on the national level and the best way to insure this was to work for a national suffrage amendment. Wilson began to lobby key members of his own party to get them to try to propose a constitutional amendment to the Constitution. The House of Representatives in January 1918 endorsed the amendment by more than the required two-thirds vote. Wilson then lobbied key members of the Senate in an effort to get the amendment proposed. He argued that the amendment was needed in the name of national security in order to facilitate the war effort. In September 1918 the Senate failed to pass the amendment by a vote of 62 to 34.

It took the end of the war in 1918 and another session of intense lobbying before the U.S. Senate finally passed the Nineteenth Amendment in May 1919. Alice Paul and others generally credit Wilson for his work in securing the final votes of key senators.[33] Moreover, Wilson continued to lobby various state legislatures and governors for adoption of the Nineteenth Amendment, which was finally ratified in August 1920.

In 1923 Alice Paul wrote the first equal rights amendment that said that equality under the law should not be abridged or denied on the basis of sex. She continued her efforts to achieve equality for women, and her activities did not escape federal authorities. In the FBI files on Alice Paul, obtained under the Freedom of Information Act, and the files on the National Woman's party, the first entry was in a listing in the General Intelligence Reporting ending February 17, 1923, as a member of a miscellaneous radical organization called the Just Government League. The report stated that the Just Government League was about to change its name to "Equal Rights," and it was supported by some of the most influential radical and semi-radical women in the country including Alice Paul. By April 21, 1923, the General Intelligence Report indicated that Alice Paul would attend a convention of the Just Government League on May 1. Moreover, by late April 1923 federal authorities brought to the attention of J. Edgar Hoover that a group called the National Council for Limitations of Arms and their powerful lobbyists, including Alice Paul, were a group that "augurs for much evil."

The National Woman's party had government coverage in its file even earlier than specific references to Alice Paul. In 1922 the FBI gathered a list of national officers and members of the national council of the party. In February 26, 1923, Hoover was informed of the following pamphlets which the National Woman's Party published:

Facts about the National Woman's Party

How Virginia Laws Discriminate Against Women

Equal Rights for Women Doctors

National headquarters of the Woman's Party

Declaration of Principles of the National Woman's Party

Outline of Campaign

Life members of the National Woman's Party

How Long Will Women Wait for Liberty

Hoover was informed that the materials would be submitted "for future reference in connection with the investigation of the various Woman's organizations." These future investigations continued with respect to Alice Paul and the National Woman's party until 1970 according to various entries into the FBI files. The last entry on the National Woman's party came in 1970 in an investigation on the women's liberation movement. Thus it appears that for almost fifty years, Alice Paul's party, which wanted equal rights for women, was deemed worthy of study by the Federal Bureau of Investigation.[34]

Presidents and Individual Rights Attorney General Mitchell Palmer's raid on civil liberties during the "Great Red Scare" of 1919–1920 also seriously calls into question Wilson's role as a defender of civil liberties. Finally, the mixed record of presidential support for civil liberties includes Franklin Roosevelt's internment of Japanese-Americans in World War II, Harry Truman's and Dwight Eisenhower's loyalty programs, and the lack of effective leadership by Truman and Eisenhower to combat McCarthyism during the second "Red Scare."

Defenders of the strong presidency would review this uneven record and acknowledge some presidential shortcomings in the defense of individual liberty. Yet they would point out that these negative examples are only aberrations in the development of presidential power that seeks generally to protect civil liberties in this country. However, the CIA/FBI revelations in 1975 and 1976 seem to indicate that presidential disregard for civil liberties in the modern presidency has become systematic behavior. In the name of "national security" U.S. presidents have ordered a wide range of programs against selected citizens. These programs directly went against First Amendment freedoms and the spirit of civil liberty protections for individual citizens.

President Lyndon Johnson was very important in giving the idea of "national security" a bad name. Johnson used the excuse of national security to further his own partisan political ambitions. He had a "passion for secrecy."[35] Chester Cooper observed, "This compulsive secrecy was not so much a conscious conspiracy as it was a reflection of the President's personal style—a style that favored a 'closed' rather than an 'open' system of policymaking.[36] Johnson used national security secrecy as an end instead of a means. As John Campbell has observed:

When the *Wall Street Journal* published speculation that the United States might bomb oil depots near Hanoi, Johnson, who had already ordered such an attack, cancelled it and launched an investigation of the bureaucracy to determine the source of the "leak." In a pattern that had been repeated before and would be repeated again, FBI agents descended on the State Department to interview all officials who were privy to the secret information.[37]

Johnson used secrecy as a means to control people. He once told reporters on his airplane, "If you play along with me I'll play along with you. . . . If you want to play it the other way, I just know how to play it both ways, too, and I know how to cut off the flow of news."[38] Johnson's love of secrecy was detailed by David Halberstam:

His was a far more structured government; decisions were made at the very top, in part because of his almost *neurotic desire for secrecy*. The more men who participate, the more gossip there is going to be, the more rumor that maybe Lyndon Johnson himself didn't make those decisions, that he needed people to make them for him, or worse, that there was disagreement at the top level of government, thus perhaps an inkling, an impression, that the decision was not perfect. *So the way to control secrecy was to control decision makers*, to keep it in as few hands as possible and make sure those hands were loyal, more committed to working with the President than anything else.[39] (emphasis added)

President Johnson needed to control every area of presidential policymaking. George Reedy said he wanted control over every little detail. James Barber outlined his compulsive handling of the bombing in Indochina, "At least from 1966 on, it was the war in Vietnam that consumed these immense energies, as Johnson pored over detailed maps to choose bombing targets and had himself awakened at three in the morning to get reports on air strikes."[40]

Johnson could not take criticism. Erwin Hargrove noted, "[Johnson] wanted no criticism at all. . . . Johnson's general style of policy decision and executive rule was to seek unanimity in government and absolute submission to his wishes."[41] He personalized his decisions. He spoke of "my boys in Vietnam," "my planes," and how he wanted to put "his hand up Ho Chi Minh's leg before Ho even knew about it."[42]

Johnson saw enemies at every corner. He said, "I can't trust anybody! What are they trying to do to me. Everybody is trying to cut me down, destroy me!"[43] David Halberstam described Johnson's paranoia, "So instead of leading, he was immobilized, surrounded, seeing critics everywhere. Critics became enemies; enemies became traitors."[44] Johnson particularly hated the press. He said, "they warp everything I do, they lie about me and what I do, they don't know the meaning of truth. They are liars and cheat."[45]

The modern president, according to Hilsman sees "obstacles and opposition, whether actual or potential, in mass publics, in the press, in Congress."[46] Johnson equated legitimate opposition with an international conspiratorial network. Richard Hofstader described this classic paranoid style as "the existence of a vast, insidious, preternaturally effective international conspiratorial network designed to perpetuate acts of the most fiendish character."[47]

Johnson hated doves on the Indochina issue, especially ones within his own presidency. He said about one dove in his administration, "Hell, he has to squat to piss."[48] Johnson's hatred of doves, his paranoia, and his passion for secrecy helped create the conditions that led to the formulation of the CIA's Operation CHAOS. According to former CIA director Richard Helms, Johnson first asked the CIA to engage in domestic surveillance to study international connections of the U.S. peace movement.[49] Johnson would repeatedly ask, "How are you getting along with your examination? Have you picked up any more information on this subject?"[50]

If Johnson abused "national security" conceptions to fit his own presidential domestic political concerns, then Richard Nixon expanded on Johnson's earlier precedent to make his conception of national security mean almost anything. As the White House transcripts revealed, Nixon consciously engaged in presidential deception by using "national security" as his "defense." Note the following tape (Conversation in Oval Office, March 21, 1973—President Nixon, Bob Haldeman and John Dean—10:12–11:55 A.M.):

President: The point is this, that it is now time, though that Mitchell has got to sit down and know where the hell all this thing stands too. You see, John is concerned, as you know, about the Ehrlichman situation. It worries him a great deal because, and this is why the Hunt problem is so serious, because it has nothing to do with the campaign. It has to do with the Ellsberg case. I don't know what the hell—(unintelligible)

Haldeman: But what I was going to say—

President: What is the answer on this? How you keep it out I don't know. You can't keep it out if Hunt talks. You see the point is irrelevant. It has gotten to this point—

Dean: *You might put it on a national security grounds basis.* (emphasis added)

Haldeman: It absolutely was.

Dean: And say that this was—

Haldeman: (unintelligible)—CIA—

Dean: Ah—

Haldeman: Seriously,

President: National Security. We had to get information for national security grounds.

Dean: Then the question is, why didn't the CIA do it or why didn't the FBI do it?

President: Because we had to do it on a confidential basis.

Haldeman: Because we were checking them.

President: Neither could be trusted.

Haldeman: It has basically never been proven. There was reason to question their position.

President: With the bombing thing coming out and everything coming out, the whole thing was national security.

Dean: *I think we could get by on that.* [emphasis added]

President: On that one I think we should simply say this was a national security investigation that was conducted and on that basis, I think the same in the drug field with Krogh. Krogh could say he feels he did not perjure himself. He could say it was a national security matter. That is why—

Dean: That is the way Bud rests easy, because he is convinced that he was doing. He said there was treason about the country, and it could have threatened the way the war was handled and (expletive deleted)—

President: Bud should just say it was a question of national security, and I was not in a position to divulge it. Anyway let's don't go beyond that.[51]

In this passage, while groping for some believable cover story, Nixon and aides stumble into the justification of "national security." Almost as an afterthought, Nixon latches onto "national security" as the reason for the activities of the White House Plumbers. In another conversation with top aide John Ehrlichman Nixon demonstrated to what lengths an agent of the president might go in the name of "national security."

President: What would you say if they said, "Did you ever do any wiretapping?" That is a question they will ask. Were you aware of any wiretapping?

Ehrlichman: Yes.

President: You would say, "Yes." Then, "Why did you do it?" You would say it was ordered on a national security basis.

Ehrlichman: National security. We had a series of very serious national security leaks.

President: As you were saying on the—

Ehrlichman: Let me go back and pick up this business about taps. I think— I have done some checking and I want you to get the feel for what I would say if this Hunt thing slopped over on me.

President: Incidentally, my view is—I don't know Hunt—I don't think Hunt will do that.

Ehrlichman: I don't think he will either, because—

President: You don't think he is going to have to take a fall for (unintelligible) any burglary? If he does—

Ehrlichman: The, the line of response would be this as I see it. Starting back in the days when I was Counsel to the President, we were very concerned with our national security leaks and we undertook at that time a whole series of steps to try and determine the source of the leaks. Some of this involved national security taps duly and properly authorized and conducted. We had three very serious breaches. After I left office of Counsel, I continued to follow this.

President: Yeah. At your request.

Ehrlichman: We had three very serious breaches. One was the whole Szulc group; one was the Pentagon Papers and the other was the Pakistan-India situation; but there were leaks all through there and so we had an active and on-going White House job using the resources of the Bureau, the Agency and the various departmental security arms with White House supervision. In this particular instance, Hunt became involved because at the time of the Pentagon Papers break we had dual concerns. We had concern about the relationship of this particular leak to other security leaks that we had across the government—Rand, etc.—and so we moved very vigorously on the whole cast of characters in the Pentagon Papers thing. Some of our findings have never come out. It was an effort to relate that incident to the other national security breaches we had, and also to find out as much as we could about this. We put a number of people into this that we had at work on other things. One was Hunt and he in turn used Liddy. I didn't know—and this is a fact—I checked this two or three ways. I didn't know what they were doing about this operation in Los Angeles until after it occurred and they came to me and told me that it had been done and that it was unsuccessful and that they were intending to make a re-entry to secure papers they were after. I said no, and stopped it at that time. Young and Krogh operated that, the whole operation. From the beginning as a matter of fact with the Szulc leaks and so on and they laid it out perfectly. And Krogh is very frank in saying "I authorized this operation in Los Angeles, no two ways about it." He says "If I am asked, that's what I will say and I will resign and leave the Department of Transportation and get out of town." He said, "I thought at the time we were doing the right thing and—"

President: Should he?

Ehrlichman: I don't think he will have to. Number one, I don't think Hunt will strike him. *If he did, I would put the national security tent over this whole operation.* [emphasis added]

President: *I sure would.* [emphasis added]

Ehrlichman: And say there are a lot of things that went on in the national interest where they involved taps, they involved entry, they involved interrogation, they involved a lot of things and I don't propose to open that up to (unintelligible) just hard line it.

President: I think that is what you have to do there. But I wanted to get that one out. OK. Go ahead.[52]

Richard Nixon believed that national security issues let the president operate outside the law. His advisor John Ehrlichman told the Senate Watergate committee that President Nixon had the "power to authorize an inherent break-in in matters concerning national security."[53] As Nixon later told David Frost, "When the president does it that means that it is not illegal." In the same interview, he also told Frost:

Frost: So what in a sense you're saying is that there are certain situations—and the Huston Plan or that part of it was one of them—where the President can decide that it's in the best interests of the nation or something, and do something illegal....

Nixon: ... Exactly. Exactly. If the President, for example approves something ... approves an action because of national security, or in this case because of a threat to internal peace and order of significant magnitude, then the President's decision in that instance is one that enables those who carry it out, to carry it out without violating a law. Otherwise they're in an impossible position.[54]

Later Nixon tried to clarify his remarks about the justifications for illegal actions by presidents when he compared himself to Abraham Lincoln's situation during the Civil War. Nixon explained to Frost:

Nixon: Well at root I had in mind I think was perhaps much better stated by Lincoln during the War Between the States. Lincoln said, and I think I can remember the quote almost exactly, he said, "Actions which otherwise would be unconstitutional could become lawful if undertaken for the purpose of preserving the Constitution and the nation."

Frost: But there was no comparison was there between the situation you faced and the situation Lincoln faced, for instance?

Nixon: This nation was torn apart in an ideological way by the war in Vietnam as much as the Civil War tore apart the nation when Lincoln was President.

Frost: But when you said, as you said when we were talking about the Huston Plan, you know, "If the President orders it, that makes it legal" as it were.... Is there anything in the Constitution or the Bill of Rights that suggests the President is that far of a sovereign, that far above the law?

Nixon: No there isn't. There's nothing specific that the Constitution contemplates in that respect... I do know this: that it has been, however, argued that as far as a President is concerned, that in wartime, a President does have certain extraordinary powers which would make acts that would otherwise be unlawful, lawful if undertaken for the purpose of preserving the nation and the Constitution which is essential for the rights we're all talking about.[55]

NATIONAL SECURITY AND CIVIL LIBERTIES

One scholar writing decades ago without the evidence of the CIA/FBI revelations could offer fairly accurate empirical hypotheses about the relationship between national security and civil liberty. The CIA/FBI revelations just add weight to the propositions John Lovell observed:

The greater the tension within the society stemming from concern about a threat to the nation—

(a) the lower will be the level of tolerance by the general public of individuals and groups whose words, deeds, or ethnic origins seem alien to established national-policy objectives.

(b) the greater will be the tendency of politicians to seek to suppress dissent from policies which purport to cope with the threat.

(c) the more limited will be the range of individual action and expression regarded as constitutionally protected by the courts.[56]

The only problem with the observations as related to the American political system is that U.S. presidents have taken the responsibility upon themselves to define who our enemies are, what threats to the national interest are, and what the response should be. Presidents have a capacity to engage in unilateral, nonreciprocal covert programs to get perceived enemies without the backing of broad-based public support and national consensus, if they so desire.

The danger that the national security system poses for individual liberty has generally been recognized in the agenda of public controversy since the aftermath of the Palmer Raids. In 1924 Attorney General Harlan Stone dictated the FBI's new position on domestic intelligence when he stated:

The Bureau of Investigation is not concerned with political or other opinions of individuals. It is concerned only with their conduct and then only with such conduct as is forbidden by the laws of the United States.... When a police system passes beyond these limits, it is dangerous to the proper administration of justice and to human liberty, which it should be our first concern to cherish.[57]

Another Attorney General Robert Jackson in 1940 noted, "Those who are in office are apt to regard as 'subversive' the activities of any of those who would bring about a change of administration."[58] Thus, the warnings against the problems of national security intrusions on civil liberties have been around for some time. Modern presidents chose not to heed the warnings.

If warnings did not provide adequate systemic protections, then the individual discretion and ethical judgments of field officers provided even less protection against civil liberties erosions. Legal and ethical issues were often overlooked by directors of covert programs. If discussion of legality did come about, the operations continued with even a tighter veil of secrecy. Yet in some cases where the directors of operations admitted the illegal or unethical nature of the activity, the directors still permitted the programs to continue.[59]

Given this system, what should we ask presidents to do to protect civil liberties while maintaining national security? Maxwell Taylor wants presidents first to recognize the legitimate claims of national security in order to protect national valuables like the Bill of Rights.[60] Richard Longaker wants presidents to take a positive step to promote civil liberties rather than protecting them through presidential restraint and indifference. Presidents would do this by following his five normative propositions: presidents *should* play a "moderating force against the ubiquitous police and military mentality of the Cold War period"; presidents *should* accept as a "constitutional necessity the participation of the Federal executive in efforts to improve the nation's record in civil rights"; presidents *should* be provided with "open channels of information in order to increase his awareness and knowledge of programmatic and individual violations of constitutional rights"; presidents *should* require for all appointments "an estimate of the value which an appointee attaches to constitutional restraints"; and finally presidents *should* "be aware that his words and acts help to build an image of official attitudes toward individual liberties."[61]

However, this normative appeal to the president's own ethical discretion would be doomed as a protection for civil liberties, given the past presidential record. Presidents need to be restrained by the rule of law, and the "tent" of national security must be lifted from civil liberties by systematic checks on the intelligence agencies and on presidents. New laws and charters must be devised.

PROSPECTS FOR THE 1990S

National security does *not* have to mean whatever the president defines it to mean, nor does national security have to mean the state "by which the dominant and achieving groups in American society organize taxation, bureaucratic, technical, and military power to support the U.S. imperial system."[62] National security activity *can* mean what the representative bodies of the polity outline it to be. The House and the Senate should adopt prohibitive charters for the FBI, the CIA, the other intelligence agencies, and the president to detail what they cannot do in the name of "national security." Constitutional checks and the rule of law are better protections for civil liberties than rule by conscience.

The prospects for CIA and FBI reform looked relatively good after the CIA/FBI revelations in 1975 and 1976. Yet the agencies were able to stall the initial stages of reform until the immediate effect of the CIA/FBI headlines faded from the public consciousness. Now as we move into the 1990s the House and Senate have still not ratified any *prohibitive* FBI or CIA charters. Moreover, the prospects for Congress passing this kind of legislation grow slimmer everyday.

Thus it appears that the tension of national security versus civil liberties is still alive and unresolved. Unless the House and Senate take prohibitive actions, the president and the intelligence communities will be operating with "business as usual." This probability bodes ill for the future of individual liberty. A more important danger signal is that most citizens have grown bored with the entire discussion of national security versus civil liberties.

NOTES

1. James M. Burns, *Presidential Government: The Crucible of Leadership* (Boston: Houghton Mifflin, 1973), p. 281.

2. Alfred Kelley and Winfred Harbison, *The American Constitution: Its Origins and Development* (New York: W. W. Norton, 1970), p. 197.

3. Leonard W. Levy, *Jefferson and Civil Liberties: The Darker Side* (Cambridge, Mass.: Harvard University Press, 1963), p. 59; see also Chap. 4.

4. Melvin Steinfield, *Our Racist Presidents: From Washington to Nixon* (San Ramon, Calif.: Consensus Publishers, 1972), p. 80.

5. Richard Longaker, *The Presidency and Individual Liberties* (Ithaca, N.Y.: Cornell University Press, 1961), p. 19.

6. Robert J. Goldstein, *Political Repression in Modern America: 1870 to Present* (New York: Schenkman Publishing, 1978), p. 67.

7. Arthur Schlesinger, Jr., ed., *The Writings and Speeches of Eugene V. Debs* (New York: Greenberg Publishers, 1948), p. 425.

8. McAlister Coleman, *Eugene V. Debs, Man Unafraid* (New York: Hermitage Press, 1930), p. 285.

9. Ibid., p. 289.

10. Ray Ginger, *The Bending Cross* (New Brunswick, N.J.: Rutgers University Press, 1949), p. 364.

11. Coleman, *Eugene V. Debs*, p. 288.

12. Schlesinger, *Writings and Speeches*, p. 418.

13. Ibid.

14. Ibid., p. 435.

15. Ibid., p. 436.

16. Amelia Fry interview with Alice Paul, "Conversations with Alice Paul: Woman Suffrage and the Equal Rights Amendment," Suffragists Oral History Project, The Bancroft Library, University of California, 1976, p. 33.

17. Sidney Bland, *Techniques of Persuasion: The National Woman's Party and Woman Suffrage, 1913–1919* (Ph.D. dissertation, George Washington University, 1972), p. 34.

18. "Lord Mayor's Feast Stoned by Women," *The New York Times*, November 10, 1909.

19. "Suffragettes Sentenced," *The New York Times*, November 11, 1909.

20. "Suffragette Tells of Forcible Feeding," *The New York Times*, February 19, 1910.

21. "Won't Try to Start Suffrage War," *The New York Times*, January 2, 1910.

22. John Davidson, ed., *A Crossroads of Freedom: The 1912 Campaign Speeches of Woodrow Wilson* (New Haven, Conn.: Yale University Press, 1956), p. 480.

23. Christine Lunardini and Thomas Knock, "Woodrow Wilson and Woman Suffrage: A New Look," *Political Science Quarterly* 95, no. 4 (Winter 1980–81): 657

24. Inez Hayes Irwin, *The Story of Alice Paul* (Fairfax, Va.: Denlinger's Publishers, 1977), p. 46.

25. Lunardini and Knock, "Woodrow Wilson and Woman Suffrage," p. 660.

26. Irwin, *Story of Alice Paul*, pp. 62–63.

27. Ibid., p. 227.

28. *Messages and Papers of the Presidents*, vol. 16 (New York: Bureau of National Literature, 1918), pp. 8375–8376.

29. "Hunger Striker Is Forcibly Fed," *The New York Times*, November 9, 1917.

30. "Force Yard of Jail to Cheer Miss Paul," *The New York Times*, November 10, 1917.

31. Ibid.

32. "White House Pickets Held without Bail," *The New York Times*, November 14, 1917.

33. Lunardini and Knock, "Woodrow Wilson and Woman Suffrage," pp. 670–671; see also Sally H. Graham, "Woodrow Wilson, Alice Paul and the Woman Suffrage Movement," *Political Science Quarterly* 98, no. 4 (Winter 1983–84): 665–679.

34. See Federal Bureau of Investigation files on Alice Paul and on the National Woman's Party available under the Freedom of Information Act from the FBI.

35. Townsend Hoopes, *The Limits of Intervention* (New York: David McKay, 1970), p. 5. See also James Barber, *The Presidential Character* (Englewood Cliffs, N.J.: Prentice-Hall, 1972), p. 94, and Erwin C. Hargrove, *The Power of the Modern Presidency* (New York: Alfred A. Knopf, 1974), p. 38.

36. Chester Cooper, *The Last Crusade: America in Vietnam* (New York: Dodd Mead, 1970), p. 416.

37. John Franklin Campbell, *The Foreign Affairs Fudge Factory* (New York: Basic Books, 1971), p. 155. See also Cooper, *The Last Crusade*, p. 416.

38. Chalmers Roberts, *First Rough Draft* (New York: Praeger, 1973), p. 229.

39. David Halberstam, *The Best and the Brightest* (Greenwich, Conn.: Fawcett Crest, 1973), p. 556.

40. George Reedy, *The Twilight of the Presidency* (New York: New American Library, 1970), p. 31; and see Barber, *The Presidential Character*, pp. 52–53.

41. Hargrove, *The Power of the Modern Presidency*, p. 38.

42. Halberstam, *The Best and the Brightest*, p. 721.

43. Barber, *The Presidential Character*, p. 53.

44. Halberstam, *The Best and the Brightest*, p. 757.

45. Barber, *The Presidential Character*, p. 54.

46. Roger Hilsman, *The Politics of Policymaking in Defense and Foreign Affairs* (New York: Harper and Row, 1971), p. 22. See also Richard Neustadt, 2d ed. *Presidential Power* (New York: John Wiley 1964).

47. Quoted in Howard Zinn, "Munich, Dominoes, and Containment," in *Trends and Tragedies in American Foreign Policy*, ed. Michael Parenti (Boston: Little, Brown, 1971), p. 180.

48. Halberstam, *The Best and the Brightest*, p. 645.

49. U.S. Senate, Select Committee on Intelligence, (Washington, D.C.: U.S. Government Printing Office, 1976), p. 100.

50. Ibid.

51. Richard Nixon's Watergate Transcripts are in the public domain. See *The White House Transcripts* (New York: Bantam Books-New York Times, 1974), pp. 163–164.

52. Ibid., pp. 236–238.

53. John Ehrlichman, Testimony Before the Select Committee on Presidential Campaign Activities of the United States Senate: Watergate and Related Activities, 93rd Congress, 1st session, Book 6 (Washington, D.C.: U.S. Government Printing Office, 1973), pp. 2599–2601.

54. Richard Nixon-David Frost Interview Transcripts, text in *Indianapolis Star*, May 20, 1977, p. 12.

55. Ibid., p. 17.

56. John Lovell, *Foreign Policy in Perspective: Strategy Adaptation, Decision Making* (New York: Holt, Rinehart and Winston, 1970), p. 338.

57. *Church Committee Final Report*, Book 2, p. 3.

58. Ibid., p. 4.

59. See Christy Mach and Susan Kaplan, *Documents* (New York: Penguin Books, 1980), pp. 40–60; and see *Church Committee Report*, Book II, pp. 137–164.

60. Maxwell D. Taylor, "The Legitimate Claims of National Security," *Foreign Affairs* 52, No. 3 (April 1974): 577–594.

61. Richard Longaker, *The Presidency and Individual Liberties* (New York: Cornell University Press, 1961), pp. 230–231.

62. Marcus Raskin, *The Politics of National Security* (New Brunswick, N.J.: Transaction Books, 1979).

3

Presidential Accountability in Controlling Intelligence

The current system for controlling intelligence agencies that grew out of the CIA/FBI revelations of 1975–76 by the Church and Pike committees dramatically failed to work for the Reagan administration. The oversight provided by the permanent intelligence committees in the House and Senate could better be described as "overlook." The system is fatally flawed. It expects an American president to share national secrets; yet, it gives the executive branch the power to define national secrets. The system expects that American presidents and representatives of the president will tell the truth and not engage in deception. When the system fails and the inevitable intelligence abuses become public, the system of accountability in the House and Senate attacks the intelligence agencies for alleged wrongdoing and fails to keep the president accountable. The system has institutionalized Frank Church's "rogue elephant" theory and investigates alleged abuses by agencies rather than holding the American president accountable for actions taken in his name.

This chapter outlines reasons why the current controls over the intelligence agencies have not worked during the administration of a popular incumbent. The analysis will focus on presidential secrecy, deception, covert domestic operations to get enemies of the administration, and covert operations to get international enemies of the administration. The message is that the president must be held accountable for these actions and he has not been called upon to account for his actions.

PRESIDENTIAL ACCOUNTABILITY REVISITED

The president of the United States is the crucial actor in the national political information system. As many observers noted, information is the key political currency in national politics. In a system based on persuasive power and the ability to get others to do what they would not ordinarily do, the person who has the most control over political information becomes the person who has the most power. The president in our system has the ability to control the most information, political intelligence, and political knowledge in the system. By information control, or the system that processes political information, the president is called upon to make decisions about the availability of information relating to what the president is doing to the Congress, the bureaucracy, the political party, the media, foreign governments, special publics, and the mass public.

Without shared information, the House and Senate intelligence committees cannot be in a position to carry out oversight responsibilities. Moreover, under the current agreements, the House and Senate Intelligence Committees can only listen to extraordinary tales of intelligence covert operations because members of the committee are bound by law not to reveal whatever outrageous operation has been revealed to them.

According to Joel Aberbach, factors that promote more oversight by Congress over the executive are "corruption, crisis, and publicity."[1] However, the oversight that should have been forthcoming after Watergate and the CIA/FBI tales of the 1970s did not set up a system that could prevent abuses of the intelligence communities in the 1980s. Franck and Weisband have observed that Congress is "voluntarily reticent" in asking the executive to account to the appropriate committees. For them, Congress has maintained:

We shall allow you to act as the judge of what may have to remain an executive secret in the field of foreign affairs, so long as we are convinced that you are keeping from us only those matters the withholding of which any reasonable Member would recognize to be absolutely essential to the national interest.[2]

The Hughes-Ryan Amendment to the 1974 Foreign Assistance Act tried to mandate a system of oversight:

No funds appropriated under the authority of this or any other Act may be expended by or on behalf of the Central Intelligence Agency for operations in foreign countries, other than activities solely for obtaining necessary intelligence, unless and until the President finds that each such operation is important to the national security of the United States and reports, in a timely fashion, a description and scope of such operation to the appropriate committees of the Congress, including the Committee on Foreign Relations of the United States Senate and the Committee on Foreign Affairs of the United States House of Representatives.[3]

Yet the Hughes-Ryan Amendment did not envision that a president would withhold information from the appropriate committees or that a president would actually lie to a committee of Congress. These powerful executive tools of secrecy and deception have allowed the president to escape accountability.

SECRECY

The president may choose to control information by using secrecy, or the process that provides a capability to keep information from others. The president may adopt the following strategies to keep information from others:

1. Withhold information from others about presidential decisions and actions
2. Use the institutionalized presidential secrecy system and classified information system
3. Conduct certain business with "no record," "for your eyes only," or by euphemistically wording instructions to subordinates in the form of codewords

In deciding what kinds of information the president may want to keep from others, the president often uses a crude costs/benefits calculus that is influenced by the need to promote legitimate "national security," the strategic advantages gained from secrecy, ongoing foreign policy commitments, the domestic political environment, and the need to conceal incompetence, inefficiency, wrongdoing, personal embarrassment, national embarrassment, and/or administrative error.

Some of the benefits that society gains by presidential secrecy are:

1. Secrecy protects the development of diplomatic negotiations by giving flexibility to advisors in the negotiating stage.
2. Secrecy protects intelligence and covert intelligence-gathering means.
3. Secrecy guards military plans, troop movements, strategy, and weapons research and development.
4. Secrecy protects treaties and agreements with other nations.
5. Secrecy guards information about other nations' defense plans, diplomatic negotiations, treaties, agreements, and intelligence reports and sources that, if disclosed, would compromise the other nation.
6. Secrecy guards the executive process by providing for a higher level of candor in the routine exchange of confidences, and it makes it easier for dissenters to attack policy from the inside without having their loyalty questioned.[4]

On the other hand, presidential secrecy may have great costs for society, such as the following:

1. Secrecy provides an internal threat to a stable balance of power by creating a class of people with a "need to know" in a system where "information is power."
2. Presidential secrecy is undemocratic, unjust, and morally wrong. It enables leadership by coercion and not persuasion.
3. Secrecy costs society by providing uncertainty in the arms race because it may allow the enemy to underestimate our real military strength.
4. Presidential secrecy creates a loss of trust and support for governmental policy when a real or imagined "credibility gap" exists.
5. Presidential secrecy fosters a climate that encourages the growth of undemocratic personality traits in leaders.
6. Secrecy inhibits scientific exchange.
7. Secrecy makes possible the corrupt conduct of foreign affairs.
8. Presidential secrecy encourages presidential lying. For one to keep a secret effectively, one must be prepared to lie.

9. Secrecy encourages the excessive leaking of confidential information, which might possibly threaten the national security.

10. Secrecy hinders free competition within the military-industrial complex and covers huge cost overruns from citizens.

11. Presidential secrecy hides dissent with the executive and obscures the administrative history of most crucial decisions.

12. Secrecy is politically unwise. The presidential secrecy system increases the chance that covert operations will be selected over other alternatives, reduces the effectiveness of such operations, hinders accurate intelligence evaluation, and distorts the executive decision-making process.[5]

When presidents select the option of secrecy in their information control policies they must be aware of these potential benefits and costs. Moreover, presidents should be aware of some of the so-called "hidden costs" of secrecy. One such important hidden cost of secrecy in the executive branch has been the cost that excessive secrecy has on the relationship between Congress and the president.

Excessive secrecy makes a farce out of the legitimate oversight function of the intelligence committees in the House and Senate. Moreover, the extreme reverence of executive secrets by members of Congress is not conducive to fulfilling the function of oversight.

The Reagan administration had a passion for secrecy. One would have to go back to the Nixon Watergate years to find a president so obsessed with keeping secrets. The Reagan administration consistently tried to limit the scope of the Freedom of Information Act. Attempts were made to exempt the Central Intelligence Agency from complying with this act. The classification system was rewritten by the Reagan administration to make information more secretive rather than more open. By Executive Order in 1982 Reagan allowed public officials to classify at the highest levels of secrecy when in doubt, rather than the lowest level of secrecy. When classifying documents, public officials were allowed to eliminate "the people's right to know" consideration. Moreover, classifiers could label at the highest levels of secrecy without having to identify the potential harm to national security.[6]

The Reagan administration proclaimed by executive fiat a policy that requires essentially lifelong prepublication censorship for most government employees. At one point, the Reagan administration threatened mandatory lie-detector tests for government workers. The CIA under the Reagan administration started charging $100 per routine search under the Freedom of Information Act to make the cost of using the "right to know" prohibitive. The Reagan Justice Department refused to release or force the FBI to release information about domestic harassment of John Lennon by the Nixon administration because it would violate "national security." Reagan signed into law the Intelligence Identities Protection Act, which prohibits the disclosure of the names of individuals involved in some way with the CIA, and it tried to stop the free flow of information by using the McCarren-Walter Act of 1952 to keep out of the United States any foreign visitors who might engage "in activities which would be prejudicial to the public interest."[7] Among the many foreign visitors who were banned for what they might communicate to the American people was Hortensia Allende, the widow of Chilean President Salvador Allende.

The Reagan administration was even so bold in trying to protect secrets that in the spring of 1986 CIA Director William Casey threatened to recommend *The Washington Post* and *Newsweek* for prosecution under an obscure 1950 statute that prohibits the disclosure of "classified information." The *Post* and *Newsweek* had published intercepts of messages between Libyan People's Bureau in East Berlin and Libyan authorities in Tripoli concerning the bombing of a West Berlin nightclub. These intercepts were supposed to be "the smoking gun" that tied the bombing to Libya and were first mentioned by President Reagan. Many independent analysts were still unable to tie a bombing conclusively to Libya after the intercepts were released, so it is little wonder that the CIA did not want them published.

DECEPTION

Another form of presidential information control is the use of deception. Presidential deception may take the form of (1) lies and "cover stories," (2) inaccurate statements and misstatements of fact, (3) symbolic manipulation, and (4) "white lies" and "the good lie." Lies and cover stories are needed to protect some of the so-called legitimate executive secrets that were discussed under potential benefits of secrecy. Cover stories also protect secretive, unilateral presidential action. When presidents and information advisors intentionally and deliberately misrepresent the facts to further their own ends, then they are engaging in presidential deception. Symbolic manipulation qualifies as deceptive information control because the administration tries to convey a false image of reality by manipulating various political symbols to the public, the media, special publics, Congress, and certain sections of the bureaucracy. Finally, "white lies" or "the good lie" also qualify as deception even though the liar is not necessarily trying to further his own ends but rather is lying for some other, higher motive.

The deception that Ronald Reagan practiced was so successful it became part of his legend rather than an extremely negative feature of his governing ability. Reagan was not good with details, facts, data, evidence, or reality. He played fast and loose with the truth during press conferences, speeches, televised addresses, and media exchanges. Reagan made so many errors, misstatements, gaffes, blunders, "bonehead" remarks, and blatant lies that Mark Green was moved to write a book about *Reagan's Reign of Error.*[8] After the bombing of the Marines in Beirut, the Reagan administration suggested that one of the reasons why the terrorists had surprised the U.S. troops was that the Carter administration had let the U.S. intelligence capabilities lapse. He suggested that the Carter administration had also let the U.S. defense and military readiness fall behind the Soviets. In 1984, candidate Reagan continued his "Carter bashing."

Reagan's veracity became an inside joke for reporters covering the White House. His statements were so obviously false on many occasions that incredulous reporters began asking White House Press Secretary Larry Speakes for clarifications after major press exchanges. The low point of this sad national joke came in 1985 when Reagan made an off-the-cuff remark about the need to recognize the Palestine Liberation Organization. When reporters rushed to Speakes for clarification he replied, "Ladies and Gentlemen, the President's statements do not reflect the policy of the Reagan administration."

The surprise bombing of Libya on April 14, 1986, added new dimensions to Reagan's imperial presidency. Since 1981 Reagan had carried on a verbal and sometimes hostile war against Muammar Qaddafi and Libya. Reagan had been elected in 1980 by promising to be tough with terrorists and to restore American pride. He portrayed Qaddafi as a "madman" and the person who was really responsible for international terrorism. Reagan challenged Qaddafi's "line of death" in the Gulf of Sirte in 1981 by sending the Sixth Fleet into these international waters. The Libyan air force attacked, and the United States responded by shooting down two Libyan planes. In August of that same year, the Reagan administration leaked to the press and then publicly announced that Libyan "hit teams" were in the United States to try to assassinate the president. Within days, Jack Anderson exposed that the story about Libyan "hit squads" in the United States was "phoney."[9]

By 1983 Americans had become targets for terrorist violence. More than 240 U.S. Marines and officials were killed in a terrorist attack on a Marine compound in Lebanon. In June 1985 a TWA jet was hijacked to Beirut, and in October 1985 the ship the *Achille Lauro* was seized. In 1985 word leaked out that the Reagan administration was working on contingency plans to assassinate Qaddafi, which, if true, would violate executive orders by Ford and Reagan that forbid employees of the U.S. government from engaging in assassination plots. Rather than deny the validity of the story, the Reagan administration said they would try to track down the source of the leak.

In December 1985 the Reagan administration announced that Qaddafi was responsible for the massacres at the Rome and Vienna airports that killed nineteen people, including five Americans. In a televised address, Reagan claimed he had "irrefutable" evidence that Libya was behind the terrorists attacks. In January 1986 the Operations Sub-Group of the National Security Council, chaired by Col. Oliver North, suggested that Tripoli be bombed in retaliation.[10] Reagan resisted, but in March 1986 he sent the Sixth Fleet to test the "line of death" again. Libyan forces fired on American planes, as the administration hoped, and the U.S. forces bombed three Libyan patrol boats and a missile site. Qaddafi responded by increasing his anti-Reagan rhetoric.

In April 1986, a West Berlin disco was bombed, and one American soldier lost his life. Reagan did not announce that he held Libya responsible, but leaks appeared in the press to set up this confrontation. Finally, Reagan launched the attack on Tripoli and Benghazi ten days after the disco attack. Reagan told the American people that U.S. intelligence had picked up coded messages from Libya that proved that Libya was responsible for the disco attack. Once again, he claimed that the evidence was "irrefutable."

Reagan's unilateral bombing attack of the headquarters of Qaddafi constituted a unilateral act of war. It violated all international conventions, the War Powers Act, and both the Ford and Reagan orders on assassination plots. West German officials were prosecuting Jordanian terrorists Nizar Hindawi and his brother for the La Belle disco bombing. The Hindawi brothers claimed that they had Syrian sponsors. Reagan's "irrefutable" evidence has been refuted by most intelligence officials in Western Europe.[11]

The last nation that Reagan tried to overthrow was Nicaragua. Since 1981, the Reagan administration had been using the Central Intelligence Agency and the American stand-in army, the Contras, to defeat Daniel Ortega and the Sandinistas. The war has been labeled as the "secret" war in Nicaragua, but it has been anything but secret. The CIA has mined harbors, issued assassination manuals, and supplied troops with intelligence, equipment, and strategy in an attempt to defeat the government in Nicaragua.[12]

The Nicaraguan war has been an American presidential war. The war continued because the Contras received the backing of the Reagan administration. Expressed administration policy was to defeat the Sandinistas. Reagan's involvement was a lie, and it was illegal. It violated every international accord and agreement with respect to aggression that the United States has made.

From 1982 to 1985 the Reagan administration systematically deceived the American people, Congress, and the media about its actual involvement in attempts to overthrow the legitimate regime of Daniel Ortega and the Sandinistas in Nicaragua. Reagan railed against state-sponsored terrorism at the same time he was funding the "freedom-fighting" Contras in their attempts to eliminate the Sandinista government.

With respect to Libya, after bombing the headquarters of Qaddafi in a surprise "retaliation" attack, Reagan maintained that he was not trying to kill Qaddafi. Within months after the attack, the administration began an official U.S. "disinformation" campaign against Qaddafi. Reagan approved a memo by Vice Admiral John Poindexter, his national security advisor, to distribute "disinformation" to destabilize the Qaddafi regime. When *The Washington*

Post received this leaked memo, the administration ordered the FBI to find the leader.[13]

The Reagan administration was prone to lie even in situations where previous presidents who had lied in similar situations finally had to tell the truth. In 1960, Dwight Eisenhower denied that the United States was flying U–2 spy flights over the Soviet Union. When the Soviets shot down a spy plane and captured pilot Gary Powers, Eisenhower finally admitted what the rest of the world knew, that the United States was flying spy flights over the Soviet Union. However, in a similar situation, Reagan refused to stop lying even after the cover of the operation had been blown. When a C–123 cargo plane was shot down over Nicaragua, the Sandinistas captured Eugene Hasenfus. The Reagan administration continued to deny that Hasenfus was connected to any "official" U.S. operation to supply the Contras.[14]

The problem with the systematic lying of the Reagan administration was that no one really seemed to care. Reagan's defense was always to the effect that the "President did not lie. And if he did, he did not mean to." As James Miller noted:

Reagan has made skillful use of the manipulative techniques of Hollywood. Employing an array of acting and script-writing cliches—the self-deprecating jokes; the heartwarming anecdote; the boyish grin; the look of principled determination; even on occasion, the catch in the voice and the hint of a tear in the eye—he has cast himself in the classic Hollywood role of the embattled Honest Politician, a role that was most memorably played by his friend Jimmy Stewart, in *Mr. Smith Goes to Washington*.[15]

Reagan's main achievement with respect to deception in American politics, according to Miller, "represents a transfer of a specific show-business objective—the willing suspension of disbelief—to politics."[16] This willing suspension of disbelief can have some serious consequences for the American public. As one of Mark A. Stamaty's cartoon characters in his *Washingtoon* comic strip said, "Haven't we learned from our president that it doesn't matter *what* our policies are. What matters is how we *feel* about ourselves and how effective we are at selling ourselves *to* ourselves and to others. Because once we achieve that level of unwavering self-esteem, *anything* we do will feel right to us. And everyone else can go to hell."[17]

THE CIA/FBI REVELATIONS

Arnold Wolfers's classic argument about national security being an ambitious symbol makes sense on one level. Wolfers noted,

When political formulas such as "national interest" or "national security" gain popularity they need to be scrutinized with particular care. They may not mean the same thing to different people. They may not have any precise meaning at all. Thus while appearing to offer guidance and a basis for a broad consensus they may be permitting everyone to label whatever policy he favors with an attractive and possibly deceptive name.[18]

However, for American presidents over the last forty years there seems to have been no ambiguity at all over the meaning of national security as it relates to internal security. *National security* and *internal security* clearly mean whatever the President wants them to mean. This certainly is not an acceptable definition to other actors in the national security system like Congress, the political parties, the courts, the media, special interest groups, and the public, but this definition supplies the operational reality for presidential behavior with respect to the intelligence community.

Other actors from 1940 to 1975 also allowed the president to create a national security system which gave him the option of ordering unilateral secretive and deceptive programs to maintain his vision of what "national security" and "internal security" should be all about even though the other actors may have had different perceptions. Thus national security and internal security have not been vague terms to the actor in the system, the president of the United States, who had the capability of initiating secretive and deceptive programs.

In 1975 and 1976 the cover for past wrongdoings by the Central Intelligence Agency and the Federal Bureau of Investigation was forever blown by the Rockefeller Commission, the Senate Select Committee on Intelligence Activities, and the House Select Committee on Intelligence Activities. In what came to be known as the CIA/FBI "revelations" (though to some citizens, particularly those against whom the secret programs were directed, the evidence was not new information), the CIA and FBI were documented as clearly attacking First Amendment freedoms. Presidential involvement, support, knowledge, and acquiescence in these programs was even more revealing.

Presidents used the FBI as a secret tool to conduct broad surveillance programs against American citizens. Although the 1924 Attorney General Harlan Stone had issued an administrative directive to abolish the political intelligence division of the FBI, it took little more than a series of secret directives from Franklin Roosevelt in 1936 to restore domestic political surveillance.[19] This restoration established the concept of presidential approval for FBI domestic political surveillance. From 1936 to 1976 the domestic surveillance by the intelligence community included the following kinds of abuses as revealed by the Church Committee:

1. *Too many people were affected by domestic intelligence activity.*

The FBI headquarters developed over 500,000 domestic intelligence files and the field offices developed many more.

Nearly a quarter of a million first class letters were opened and photographed in the U.S. by the CIA between 1953 and 1973.

At least 130,000 first class letters were opened by the FBI between 1940–1966 in eight U.S. cities.

Some 300,000 individuals were indexed in a CIA computer system and separate files were created on approximately 7,200 Americans and over 100 domestic groups during the course of CIA's Operation CHAOS (1967–1973).

2. *Too much information was collected for too long.*

The women's liberation movement was infiltrated by informants who collected material about the movement's policies, leaders and individual members.

3. *Too much covert action and the use of illegal and improper means.*

The FBI's COINTELPRO—counter intelligence program—was designed to "disrupt" groups and "neutralize" individuals deemed to be threats to domestic security.

COINTELPRO tactics included:

Anonymously attacking the political beliefs of targets in order to induce employers to fire them;

Anonymously mailing letters to the spouses of intelligence targets for the purpose of destroying their marriages;

Obtaining from IRS the tax returns of a target and then attempting to provoke an IRS investigation for the express purpose of deterring a protest leader from attending the Democratic National Convention;

Falsely and anonymously labelling as Government informants members of groups known to be violent, thereby exposing the falsely labelled member to expulsion or physical attack.

From "late 1963" until his death in 1968, Martin Luther King, Jr., was the target of an intensive campaign by the FBI to "neutralize" him as an effective civil rights leader. The FBI gathered information about Dr. King's plans and activities through an extensive surveillance program, employing nearly every intelligence-gathering technique at the Bureau's disposal, to use to discredit King.

The program to destroy King as the leader of the Civil Rights movement included efforts to discredit him with his wife, the Executive branch, Congressional leaders, foreign heads of state, American ambassadors, churches, universities, and the press.

Since the early 1930s, intelligence agencies have frequently wiretapped and bugged American citizens without the benefit of judicial warrant.

Warrantless break-ins have been conducted by intelligence agencies since World War II.[20]

After reviewing these kinds of abuses the Church Committee noted the adverse effects on individual liberty that the intelligence community posed for American citizens. The CIA and FBI under presidential leadership was engaged in a general effort to discredit selected citizens, manipulate the media, distort data to influence government policy and public perceptions, "chill" First Amendment Rights, and prevent the free exchange of ideas.[21]

PRESIDENTIAL INVOLVEMENT

U.S. presidents did not remain innocent bystanders as their intelligence agencies were running rampantly out of control. They gave secret directives, approved some programs, condoned others, and generally set the tone for the environment under which the agencies would work. Franklin Roosevelt asked J. Edgar Hoover and the FBI for more systematic intelligence collection about "subversive activities in the United States, particularly Fascism and Communism."[22] The president wanted a general outline of the movements and a report on how they may affect "the economic and political life of the country as a whole."[23] He also asked the FBI to start a file on citizens who sent telegrams to the White House opposing his national defense policy and supporting Col. Charles Lindbergh's America First Committee.[24]

Harry Truman issued a directive to the FBI acknowledging that it had the right to conduct investigations into "subversive" activities in 1950. Yet no one was prepared to define just what "subversive" meant. Moreover, Truman received inside information from the FBI about a labor union's negotiating plans and the publishing plans of some journalists.[25] Truman's Attorney General Thomas Clark even made contingency plans for the emergency detention of "potentially dangerous" persons as supplied by the FBI, by suspending the writ of habeas corpus.[26] Truman also issued a directive authorizing warrantless wiretaps by the FBI on "subversive activity here at home" and in cases "vitally affecting the domestic security."[27] He also initiated the practice of using the FBI to investigate federal employees in compliance with his executive order that established a loyalty and security program in 1947.

Dwight Eisenhower continued to use the FBI to investigate individuals in compliance with his loyalty program executive orders, and he issued a directive in 1953 that continued to give the FBI the right to engage in domestic political surveillance by charging the agency to keep track of "subversives." Eisenhower received the standard FBI-Hoover bits of information from "confidential" sources that were useful politically, and Eisenhower's Attorney General Herbert Brownell worked out an agreement with the FBI by which black bag jobs would be considered *illegal* but not *unconstitutional!*[28]

The Kennedy administration continued to receive the Hoover morsels of political trivia including information from FBI wiretaps on executive officials, a congressional staff member, a Washington law firm, a lobbyist, and a congressman.[29] Most important, the Kennedy administration gave the FBI and Hoover permission to place a "national security" wiretap on Dr. Martin Luther King, Jr., and the Southern Christian Leadership Conference (SCLC) office in 1962. Attorney General Robert Kennedy also received constant reports from Hoover on the results of the FBI's domestic surveillance of King, which was done in an effort to prove that the civil rights movement was infiltrated by Communists. Although the wiretaps and the domestic surveillance revealed no infiltration of SCLC by the Communists and no Communist influences on King, the FBI continued monitoring King's activities. The Kennedy administration did not move to stop this harassment of King by the FBI.[30]

Lyndon Johnson asked the FBI to supply him with information about his antiwar critics, and the FBI even conducted "name checks" of members of Johnson's 1964 political opponent Barry Goldwater's staff. Johnson also learned of the FBI's, particularly Hoover's, hatred of King and the programmatic response that this hatred was taking. Like Kennedy, Johnson did nothing to call Hoover off his mission of discrediting and harassing King, the 1964 Nobel Peace Prize winner. Johnson also requested purely political intelligence reports from the FBI on his critics in the Senate, and he obtained political intelligence from FBI electronic surveillance of his own 1964 Democratic National Convention.[31] Most important, Johnson issued instructions to Hoover in 1965 to find out to what extent subversives were responsible for antiwar activity. This order was directly translated as presidential approval for increased COINTELPRO action against antiwar groups.

Richard Nixon used the FBI and the CIA in the traditional manner as set by previous presidential precedent to spy on his critics. He tried to use the CIA for his own partisan political concerns, and he used the FBI in a program of electronic surveillance against certain citizens in direct violation of their constitutional rights.[32] He used the Internal Revenue Service to obtain potentially embarrassing information on his political opposition. Yet Nixon was not content with just operating within the normal parameters of presidential use of intelligence agencies to spy on citizens. He established his own version of a White House secret police, the "Plumbers," and once signed approval to the Huston Plan, a program designed to coordinate and expand domestic intelligence for the president.

The "Plumbers" used a wide range of tactics to stop so-called "national security" leaks and to discredit and harass Nixon's "enemies," most notably Daniel Ellsberg. Their exploits are now legendary.[33] The Huston Plan was developed to give the president a centralized evaluation of domestic intelligence and a broader network of information about antiwar groups. Some members of the Nixon administration and specifically Tom Charles Huston felt that the FBI and CIA efforts were inadequate in this area. Huston's plan recommended that the president approve the following:

1. Coverage by the National Security Agency of the communications of U.S. citizens using international facilities

2. Intensification of electronic surveillances and penetrations directed at individuals and groups who "pose a major threat to the internal security" and at foreign nationals in the United States of interest to the intelligence community

3. Removal of restrictions on "legal" mail coverage and relaxation of restrictions on covert coverage (mail opening) on selected targets of priority foreign intelligence and internal security interest

4. Modification of present restrictions on surreptitious entry to allow procurement of vitally needed foreign cryptographic material and to permit selective use against high priority internal security targets

5. Relaxation of present restrictions on the development of campus sources to permit expanded coverage of violence-prone and student-related groups

6. Increased coverage by CIA of American students (and others) traveling or living abroad

7. Appointment of a permanent committee consisting of the FBI, CIA, NSA, DIA, and the military counterintelligence agencies to evaluate domestic intelligence and to carry out the other objectives specified in the report.[34]

In his recommendation to H. R. Haldeman in July 1970, Huston noted that opening mail was clearly illegal but he felt the advantages to be derived from its use outweighed the risks. Moreover, with respect to surreptitious entry he warned,

use of this technique is clearly illegal; *it amounts to burglary*. It is also highly risky and could result in great embarrassment if exposed. However, it is also the most fruitful tool and can produce the type of intelligence which cannot be obtained in any other fashion.[35] [emphasis added]

Nixon approved this plan but withdrew his support five days later when J. Edgar Hoover complained about its legality. After all, the FBI did these things already.

In 1981, only five years after the Church Committee report on the abuses of the FBI and the CIA with respect to the rights of Americans, Reagan issued an executive order that gave the agencies the kind of powers that hitherto had been considered abuses. The order gave intelligence agencies the power to infiltrate domestic groups under investigation when the government had probable cause to believe that the group was acting on behalf of a foreign country. This set the stage for covert harassment of peace groups once again. The order allowed the CIA for the first time to collect foreign intelligence in the United States by "surreptitiously questioning the citizenry."[36] As Walter Karp observed,

It also authorizes the CIA to employ the entire local police force of the country in this undercover questioning, which can take place in a barroom, a barbershop, or the aisle of a K-Mart—as if the U.S. government needed to monitor the unguarded conversations of private citizens to keep itself informed about foreign countries. Getting the government off the backs of the people is the very last thing this administration wants.[37]

The Center for Constitutional Rights in New York compiled an extensive list of incidents where Central American peace activists were harassed by the FBI, the Internal Revenue Service (IRS), and other American officials. From 1983 to 1986, the center listed more than twenty-five domestic political groups that opposed Reagan's war in Nicaragua and whose offices were broken into.[38] Many groups have complained of domestic surveillance by the government, and the Sojourners, a group of religious people who have consistently opposed Reagan's war in Nicaragua, have maintained that they have been infiltrated by the FBI. Another group, the Committee in Support of the People in El Salvador, was successfully infiltrated from 1981 to 1984 by an FBI informant named Frank Varelli.[39] Many peace activists who have visited Nicaragua complained that the IRS ordered tax audits shortly after their return to the United States.

Under Justice Department guidelines issued to the FBI in 1983, the agency was allowed to collect "publicly available information" on any American it so chooses for whatever reasons it so chooses. For the Reagan administration, it was as if the CIA/FBI revelations of wrongdoing with respect to unnecessary domestic political spying as revealed by the Church and Pike Committee reports had never happened. It was business as usual for intelligence agencies who wanted to get enemies of presidential policies.

IRANGATE

In November 1986 the American news media started to pick up on a story that had been circulating in Mideast newspapers about the U.S. attempts to sell arms to Iran in order to gain the release of American hostages held in Lebanon. By February 1987 the basic outlines of the story emerged along with the startling revelation that some of the profits from the arms deal went to the Contras in Nicaragua.

The Reagan administration sold millions of dollars of military equipment to Iran, a nation that Reagan once called "Murder Incorporated," in order to secure the release of American hostages. This news violated the publicly stated neutrality of the United States in the Iraq-Iran War and it violated the Export Administration Act of 1979, which restricts exports to terrorist-supporting nations. The news violated the public understanding of Reagan's policy against terrorism. Reagan had tried to appear tough and consistent against terrorism. He said the United States would never pay ransom for hostages. Then he tried to get the Ayatollah Khomeini regime, the same regime that held America "hostage" in 1979 and 1980 during the Carter administration, to use its influence to gain the release of American hostages. In order for Iran to do this, Reagan had to supply military weapons. The president complied.

In late November 1986, Attorney General Edwin Meese announced that part of the money from the Iranian arms deal was diverted to the Contras in Nicaragua. This was the first time that Reagan claimed he ever heard of that diversion of funds. The story widened, and the key players were named, including former national security advisors Robert McFarlane, John Poindexter, and National Security Council troubleshooter, Lieut. Col. Oliver North. Then the role of Secretary of State George Shultz and Secretary of Defense Caspar Weinberger in the matter was detailed. Former White House Chief of Staff Donald Regan came under fire for letting such a deal happen and the National Security Council (NSC) and the CIA came under intense public reprobation for the ordeal.

There is evidence that the following laws may have been violated:

1. Criminal laws prohibiting conspiracy to defraud the U.S. government
2. The Export Administration Act that prohibits trade with terrorist nations
3. The Arms Export Control Act, which prohibits military assistance to countries that support international terrorism
4. Hughes-Ryan Amendment to Foreign Assistance Act of 1974 that requires presidential authorization and notification of CIA covert operations to appropriate committees of Congress
5. The Boland Amendment, which prohibited federal agencies from providing direct or indirect military aid to the Nicaragua rebels between October 1984 and October 1986
6. The Intelligence Oversight Act of 1980, which requires congressional notification of covert operations.[40]

In all this, the crucial points were what did the president authorize and when did he authorize it? How was the president involved in these matters? What did he forget? The imperial president was involved in excessive secrecy in trying to keep the "Irangate" affair from the public. The deception centered around the cowboy exploits of Oliver North and the NSC operations. The Reagan administration deceived Congress, the media, and the American public as to their actions with respect to Iran and Nicaragua. The imperial president was so isolated that he was even removed from the operations of his staff and his National Security Council. The support of the Contras with Iranian money continued the president's policy of unilateral warmaking in Nicaragua. Finally, the Irangate affair showed the arrogance, lawlessness, and lack of accountability of the Reagan administration.[41]

If Reagan headed a parliamentary democracy, his administration would have folded after Irangate. In American presidential politics, Reagan had to ride the fine line between the commitment of impeachable offenses or just plain stupidity. Reagan maintained "plausible deniability" in the whole matter by appearing as if he blundered an inept policy decision. However, Reagan is responsible for more than just a blunder. Regardless of the testimony of Poindexter and North to the various investigating agencies, the blame for Irangate must go the president of the United States. Reagan allowed a shadow American government to be set up to carry out projects that the president knew he had no authority to engage in, under current United States law and tradition. This secret antigovernment was composed of international drug and arms dealers, middle men, ex-CIA agents, retired military officials, radical right-wing patriots, investing capitalists, mercenaries, gun runners, and thrill seekers. This is hardly the government that the bicentennial of the United States Constitution was supposed to be celebrating in 1987.

Some observers have noted the similarities between Watergate and Irangate. They usually note that Irangate is not as serious a problem for democracy as Watergate posed. They are wrong. Irangate with its international secret shadow government poses more serious problems for democracy than even Richard Nixon's usurpations of presidential power. Yet few wanted the resignation of the president, and still fewer called for his impeachment. Republicans and Democrats alike said they wanted to preserve the presidency and that it would hurt America to attack a popular old president when he was down. Poor Nixon, if he had only been well liked, perhaps he might have escaped the wrath of Watergate.

If Nixon's secret White House tapes revealed the inner workings of his administration, then the Tower Commission Report did the same thing for the Reagan administration when it published messages from the "PROF" interoffice computer mail system for Reagan's National Security Council. In one memo Robert McFarlane told Oliver North,

Roger Ollie. Well done—if the world only knew how many times you have kept a semblance of integrity and gumption to US policy, they would make you Secretary of State. But they can't know and would complain if they did—such is the state of democracy in the late 20th century.[42]

With respect to whether President Reagan knew about Oliver North's secret operations in Central America, one PROF was quite revealing. North wrote John Poindexter on May 16, 1986,

I have no idea what Don Regan does or does not know re my private U.S. operation but the President obviously knows why he has been meeting with several select people to thank them for their "support for Democracy" in CentAM.[43]

The Reagan administration's secret foreign policy was clearly conducted on the unilateral imperial authority of President Reagan. His attempts to defeat the Sandinista government with military force defied the will and law of the United States Congress. Yet Reagan is not regarded as a lawbreaker. Faced with the choice of believing Ronald Reagan to be a criminal imperial president or an incompetent, lazy, hands-off president, most American opinion leaders selected the latter.[44]

Irangate ended Reagan's six-year run as "imperial president." It was a long run as imperial presidencies go. The period 1981–86 represented an upswing in presidential power in relation to Congress, the media, and public opinion.[45] One has to go back to the Franklin Roosevelt presidency to find six consecutive years of continual presidential aggrandizement. Truman and Eisenhower never enjoyed such a long period of presidential ascendancy. Lyndon Johnson and Richard Nixon each had five years of imperial presidential power before the events of Vietnam and Watergate caught up with each president respectively.

Reagan's run was so successful because of his tremendous popularity and because few recognized the signs of the imperial presidency in Reagan's actions. He offered an upswing in presidential power to a public that was ready to buy into that dream. He offered a return to an idealized past. He offered credibility, pride, patriotism, and rebirth of the American spirit. He offered the illusion of presidential competence. Most citizens purchased the entire package deal. Now there is no way to return the package, so citizens will have to wait until the next cycle of presidential power with a new reminder, "Watch out for the friendly imperial president."

Unless a political system is willing to hold the president accountable, it cannot discuss ways to keep the intelligence community under control. The record of the so-called "intelligence abuses" of the past forty years has been a record of the intelligence services carrying out the desires of the president. Until the intelligence committees contest the president for information about operations and until members of Congress feel free to discuss operations with members of the executive, then the prospects for control of the intelligence communities are not good. Given the cycle of presidential power, one might fully expect to read about the excesses of the FBI and CIA in the late 1990s.

PRESIDENTS AND NATIONAL SECURITY

National security is a genuine competing value in the process of value allocation in a democratic polity. Indeed, if a nation is not secure from *external* threats as well as being secure from legitimate *internal* threats, then the other values that a democratic polity tries to maximize will greatly suffer or cease to exist at all. Yet what values in a democratic system are to be secured by a national security system? Among the quintessential values that presidents must try to secure in a democracy are freedom of speech, freedom of press, freedom to articulate grievances, rights to privacy, freedom from government harassment, freedom of the free flow of information, freedom from government manipulation and deception, and freedom to organize politically. Ironically, when presidents seek to keep the political system secure from perceived external and internal threats, they usually minimize the quintessential democratic values at the expense of maximizing "economic stability," "domestic political stability," "international order," and most important for some presidents "incumbent presidential domestic political power advantages."

Recent presidents have given "national security" a bad name. This legitimate concept has fallen on hard times essentially because presidents have systematically used the "national security" cover to mean whatever they desire it to mean. Too often in the past national security has been used as an acceptable value to maximize in order to diminish legitimate dissent and to crush domestic political opposition. By allowing presidents to control a secret national security system, the polity has given presidents the duty to maintain *internal security* and has greatly increased the chance that the president will perceive his legitimate opponents as a threat to the nation's (his) continued survival.

There must be some check on executive power. There must be some institutional arrangements that do not allow the imperial president to run rampantly out of control. There must be someone who will tell the emperor that he has no clothes. This is a central point for understanding democratic accountability. Who shall watch the king? Who will tell the leader that he is breaking the law? What implications and consequences will the leader suffer if he breaks the law? How can we build a system that will check lawless executive behavior?

Americans have been wary of executive power ever since the American Revolution of 1776 against the tyranny of executive power of the king. Indeed in the Articles of Confederation, the first agreement on how to organize the United States, there was no strong centralized chief executive at all. Congress would control all executive power any nation needed. After the agreement on the Articles of Confederation began to fall apart precisely because there was no strong central chief executive power that could deal with crises to established order like Shay's (farmer-tax) Rebellion in Massachusetts, the elite framers assembled in Philadelphia to amend the Articles of Confederation. At the convention the framers quickly decided to throw out the entire document and to propose a new constitution for the United States. This constitution would create some balance with the problem of executive power. It would not be absolute as in monarchial executive power, and it would not be almost nonexistent as in the Articles.

The framers had some experience with executive authority. They had lived under the king, and they had been influenced by the writings of John Locke, Charles-Louis Montesquieu, and Sir William Blackstone with respect to the behavior of executives. Moreover, the framers had experience with executive authority in revolutionary state constitutions and the powers given to governors in various states, especially in New York State.

The key decisions that the framers made were that executive power would be separated from legislative and judicial power, and that executive power would be checked and balanced by other institutions of government. The executive would be accountable for his actions. In this system then, there could be no possible way for a "kinglike" executive to rule in an imperial fashion.

But how does one check a friendly, personable, popular imperial president? Writers on the imperial presidency have not often considered this problem. Ronald Reagan was not mean-spirited like Richard Nixon, and he did not have the passionate underside to his personality that Lyndon Johnson had. How then does one deal with the problem of an imperial presidency when it is not even recognized that such a condition exists? The first step is to detail the existence of the situation.[46]

The Reagan administration, besides showing excessive secrecy, deception, isolation and trappings, media manipulation, anti–civil libertarian posturing, unilateral warmaking, and arrogance, engaged in lawless and unaccountable executive behavior. The Libya, Grenada, and Nicaragua excursions violated international law. By operating in an excessively secretive and deceptive manner, Reagan escaped accountability. By using his extraordinary abilities to manipulate the media and to use his powers to persuade, he dodged responsibility.

NOTES

1. Joel D. Aberbach, "The Development of Oversight in the United States Congress: Concepts and Analysis," paper delivered at the 1977 Annual Meeting of the American Political Science Association, Washington, D.C., September 1–4, 1977, pp. 4–8. See also Robert Harmel, "Congressional Responses to Executive Privilege," 1977 American Political Science Association Annual Meeting, Washington, D.C., September 1–4, 1977; Seymour Scher, "Conditions for Legislative Control," *Journal of Politics* August 1963, pp. 526–551; Morris Ogul, *Congress Oversees the Bureaucracy* (Pittsburgh, Penn.: University of Pittsburgh Press, 1976); John F. Bibby, "Oversight—Congress' Neglected Function: Will Watergate Make a Difference?" paper delivered at the 1974 Meeting of the Western Political Science Association; and see Joseph Harris, *Congressional Control of Administration* (Washington, D.C.: Brookings Institute, 1964).

2. Thomas Franck and Edward Weisband, eds., *Secrecy and Foreign Policy* (New York: Oxford University Press, 1974), p. 427.

3. 22 USC 2422, Sec. 662. Limitation on Intelligence Activities.

4. Franck and Weisband, *Secrecy and Foreign Policy*, pp. 8–9.

5. Thomas I. Emerson, "The Dangers of State Secrecy," in *Watergate and the American Political Process*, ed. Ronald Pynn (New York: Praeger Publishers, 1975), pp. 59–60. See also Martin McGuire, *Secrecy and the Arms Race* (Cambridge, Mass.: Harvard University Press, 1965), p. 214; Francis Rourke, *Secrecy and Publicity* (Baltimore, Md.: Johns Hopkins University Press, 1961), p. 223; James Wiggins, *Freedom or Secrecy* (New York: Oxford University Press, 1956), p. 113; Arthur M. Cox, *The Myths of National Security* (Boston: Beacon Press, 1975), p. 84; David Wise, *The Politics of Lying* (New York: Vintage Books, 1973); Daniel Ellsberg, *Papers on the War* (New York: Pocket Books, 1972); and see Morton Halperin and Jeremy Stone, "Secrecy and Covert Intelligence Collection and Operation," in, *None of Your Business*, ed. Norman Dorsen and Stephen Gillers (New York: Penguin, 1975), pp. 110–111.

6. Floyd Abrams, "The New Effort to Control Information," *The New York Times Magazine*, September 25, 1983, p. 25.

7. Ibid., p. 23. See also "U.S. Still Blacklists 3,000 Canadians for Politics," *The New York Times*, February 19, 1984.

8. Mark Green and Gail MacColl, *There He Goes Again: Ronald Reagan's Reign of Error* (New York: Pantheon, 1983).

9. Tom Bower, "Was the Bombing of Tripoli a Misguided Vendetta by Reagan?" *The Listener*, April 2, 1987, p. 4.

10. Ibid., p. 5.

11. Ibid., p. 6.

12. "The Illegal War Against Nicaragua," *Center for Constitutional Rights* (New York: December 1983); Joel Brinkley, "C.I.A. Primer Tells Nicaraguan Rebels How to Kill," *The New York Times*, October 17, 1984; Philip Taubman, "President's 'Secret War' in Nicaragua Backfires," *The New York Times*, April 15, 1984, Section 4, p. 1; Lou Cannon and Don Oberdorfer, "The Mines, the CIA and Shultz's Dissent," *Washington Post National Weekly Edition*, April 23, 1984, pp. 16–17; and Philip Taubman, "U.S. Officials Say C.I.A. Helped Nicaraguan Rebels Plan Attacks," *The New York Times*, October 16, 1983, p. 1.

13. "Editors Protest to White House," *The New York Times*, October 13, 1986, p. A 11; James Reston, "How to Fool the People," *The New York Times*, October 5, 1986, p. 21 E; and Anthony Lewis, "The Reasons for Lying," *The New York Times*, October 13, 1986, p. A19.

14. Lewis, "The Reasons for Lying," p. A19.

15. James Nathan Miller, "Ronald Reagan and the Techniques of Deception," *The Atlantic Monthly*, February 1984, p. 68.

16. Ibid.

17. Mark Alan Stamaty, "Washingtoon," cartoon strip, *The Village Voice*, October 28, 1986, p. 7.

18. Arnold Wolfers, "National Security as an Ambiguous Symbol," *Political Science Quarterly* 67, no. 4 (December 1952).

19. Morton Halperin, Jerry Berman, Robert Borosage, and Christine Marwick, *The Lawless State: Crimes of the U.S. Intelligence Agencies* (New York: Penguin Books, 1976), p. 95.

20. *Church Committee Report*, Book 2, "Intelligence Activities and the Rights of Americans," pp. 5–13.

21. *Church Committee Report*, Book 2, pp. 15–18.

22. Ibid., p. 25.

23. Ibid.

24. Ibid., p. 9.

25. Ibid., p. 51.

26. Ibid., p. 54.

27. Ibid., p. 60.

28. David Wise, *The American Police State* (New York: Random House, 1976), p. 152.

29. *Church Committee Report*, Book 2, p. 9.

30. See Halperin, *The Lawless State*, pp. 61–89; and see *Church Committee Final Report*, Book 3, "Supplementary Detailed Staff Reports, Dr. Martin Luther King, Jr.: Case Study," pp. 79–184.

31. *Church Committee Final Report*, Book 2, p. 9.

32. Wise, *The American Police State*, pp. 274–321; and Halperin, *The Lawless State*, pp. 59–132.

33. *The Final Senate Watergate Report* (The Ervin Committee) (New York: Dell, 1974), pp. 64–71.

34. *Church Committee Final Report*, Book 2, p. 113.

35. Ibid., p. 114.

36. Walter Karp, "Liberty Under Siege," *Harper's*, November 1985, p. 56.

37. Ibid.

38. James Ridgeway, "Home Is Where the Covert Action Is: Harassment of Peace Groups Raises Questions," *The Village Voice*, December 16, 1986, p. 24.

39. Ibid.

40. Robert Pear, "Assembling Some of the Pieces of the Puzzle," *The New York Times*, December 14, 1986, Section 4, pp. 1–2, and see James M. McCormick and Steven S. Smith, "The Iran Arms Sale and the Intelligence Oversight Act of 1980," *PS* 20, no. 1 (Winter 1987): 29–37.

41. "High Crimes and MisDemeanors," *Mother Jones*, February/March, 1987, pp. 6–7; Pete Hamill, "Body Bag of Lies," *The Village Voice*, December 30, 1986, p. 10; Keith Schneider, "North's Record: A Wide Role in a Host of Sensitive Projects," *The New York Times*, January 3, 1987, p. 1; Fred Halliday, "Reagan's Doctrine of Deceit," *The Guardian*, February 13, 1987, p. 11; Michael Binyon, "Testimony Changed by Reagan," *The Times* (London), February 20, 1987, p. 1; Seymour Hersh, "Target Gadaffi: Reagan's Secret Plot," *Sunday Times* (London), February 22, 1987, p. 11; Alex Brummer and Mark Tran, "Irangate Cover-up Charge," *The Guardian*, February 23, 1987, p. 30; Alex Brummer, "Poindexter to Admit Briefing Reagan," *The Guardian*, March 9, 1987, p. 1.

42. *The Tower Commission Report* (New York: Bantam Books, 1987), p. 254.

43. Ibid., p. 287.

44. See *The Tower Commission Report*; William Greider, "The Lonesome Drifter," *Rolling Stone*, March 12, 1987, pp. 25–26; Simon Hoggart, "The Zombie President," *The Observer*, March 1, 1987, p. 11; "When Muddling Through Is Called Triumph," *The Guardian*, March 21, 1987, p. 14; Gail Sheehy, "Reality? Just Say No: The President's Denial Syndrome," *The New Republic*, March 30, 1987, pp. 16–18; but for articles

that do not excuse Reagan's so-called "management style," see David Bromwich, "Contragate: The Swill of Empire," *Dissent*, Spring 1987, pp. 133–135; Irving Howe, "Reagangate: The Farce and the Shame," *Dissent*, Spring 1987, pp. 136–138; Joanne Barkan, "A Cheer for the Constitution," *Dissent*, Spring 1987, pp. 138–140; and see Mark Sinker, "Arms and the Old Man," *New Musical Express*, April 11, 1987, p. 34.

45. Michael Genovese, "The Return of the Imperial Presidency," *Presidency Research Newsletter*, Winter 1986.

46. See Bob Woodward, *Veil: The Secret Wars of the CIA 1981–1987* (New York: Simon and Schuster, 1987); Leslie Cockburn, *Out of Control* (New York: Atlantic Monthly Press, 1987); *Report of the Congressional Committees Investigating Iran-Contra Affair* (New York: Times Books, 1988); Scott Armstrong and the National Security Archive, *The Chronology* (New York: Warner Books, 1987); William Blum, *The CIA: A Forgotten History* (London: Zed Books, 1986); and see Glenn Hastedt, "Covert Action" in his *American Foreign Policy* (Englewood Cliffs, N.J.: Prentice-Hall, 1988), pp. 233–254.

4

Exercise of the President's Discretionary Power in the Criminal Justice Policy Arena

To transpose an old cliché, awareness of the president's discretionary power may be so overwhelming that we haven't seen the "trees for the forest." This chapter will survey the vast amount of discretionary power that the president has in the administration of justice within the United States in order to explore some of the "trees" in the president's monumental discretionary forest.

The survey will not be confined to the limited and formal legal powers that the president has in criminal justice, although these will be highlighted. This analysis will take a broader view of presidential discretionary power, which includes the informal powers within the criminal justice arena. Power is being used loosely in the Dahlian sense where power is the ability of A (in this case, the president) to get B (some target for action within the administration of justice) to do something that B would not ordinarily do.[1] Discretionary powers, then, imply powers left to the president, which rely on judgmental decisions for arbitrary actions.

At least within the criminal justice arena, presidential power is much more than just "the power to persuade."[2] It is also the ability of the president to issue unilateral, nonreciprocal commands that gain compliance through means other than the president's persuasive powers. In short, presidents can gain compliance for their arbitrary decisions within the criminal justice arena via notions of duty, pride, role conception, conscience, interpersonal identification, coercion, and symbolic attachments that are notoriously non-reciprocal.[3]

Discretion exists "whenever the effective limits on . . . power leave . . . one free to make a choice among possible courses of action or inaction."[4] Given the scope of presidential power, the elasticity of the concept of "executive power," and the multitude of political contingencies in which the president of the United States operates, it is evident that the president can, and does, exercise vast discretion.

From the perspective of a decentralized, fragmented local-level criminal justice subsystem, the president's highly visible role as chief law enforcer with a panoply of appointive and fiscal power may appear to constitute a monolithic and powerful influence on criminal justice in America. Such a simplistic, and to some extent attractive, view was encouraged when "law and order" was politicized into a volatile presidential campaign issue in 1968. One of the most ironic questions about Watergate is whether there would have been such a massive, politically debilitating reaction to revelations about Richard Nixon's "shortcomings" as chief law enforcer had he not previously used such strong rhetoric against law violators. "Nobody," he said emphatically, "is above the law." He intimated that as president, *he* could control crime. Thomas Cronin aptly remarked, "Richard Nixon sometimes gave the impression back in 1968 that he was running for national sheriff."[5]

Granted that no one, at least theoretically, is *above* the law in America, many do often make decisions and act *beyond* the law. William Pitt said, "Where the law ends tyranny begins." But as Kenneth Culp Davis observed in *Discretionary Justice: A Preliminary Inquiry*, "Where law ends, discretion begins, and the exercise of discretion may mean either beneficence or tyranny, either justice or injustice, either reasonableness or arbitrariness."[6] Davis holds that "those who exercise governmental power are much more occupied with discretion than with law."

The ability of a president to make discretionary choices which appear to project the law and right, beneficence and justice, and *reasonableness* is central to the positive exercise of discretion. "Positive" is meant in the sense of affirming established values toward the end of justice, social equity, and fundamental fairness. Such ability may be a function of political sensitivity. Or it may be a consequence of fortuitous circumstances. Whether there have been signal differences among presidents in the way they have used discretion, or whether differential discretion is largely a matter of perception, is debated.

The purpose of this exploratory chapter is to consider the ways in which the exercise of the president's discretionary power may influence criminal justice policy. The relationship of this research to the existing work on the presidency can be explained by noting that, broadly speaking, there are three distinct approaches or levels of analysis reflected in the literature on the presidency: the traditional approach, based upon examination of the legal foundations of presidential powers and a review of historical precedents; the behavioral approach, which includes a search of the dynamics of political action and an attempt to explain the impact of particular personality and character types on national politics, and the policy analysis approach, which seeks to identify and assess the impact of presidential decisions and actions on policy outcomes. All three approaches will be drawn from in this initial inquiry into the effect of presidential discretion on the criminal justice system.

FORMAL POWERS WITHIN CRIMINAL JUSTICE

Article II, Section 1, of the U.S. Constitution states, "The executive power shall be vested in a President." Section 2, grants the President power to grant "reprieves and Pardons ... except in cases of impeachment," and Section 3 specifies that the president "shall take care that the Laws be faithfully executed." These sections, combined with other affirmative grants of power to the president, establish formal presidential powers within criminal justice. Yet by implication these formal powers create, as Arthur S. Miller has noted, "a vessel into which Chief Executives can pour almost anything they wish—or, rather, anything that the operation of the political process permits them to get away with. Nowhere is this better seen than in the area of enforcement of the laws."[7]

DISCRETION AND THE "FAITHFUL EXECUTION OF THE LAWS"

Perhaps the most crucial aspect of the president's exercise of discretionary power in criminal justice is the *way* that the president chooses that he will "faithfully" execute the laws of the land. The law that the president is obliged to enforce clearly includes the criminal laws of the United States. Acting Attorney General Bork, during Senate Judiciary Committee hearings, stated that the Constitution lodges "complete control over criminal prosecutions" in the executive branch.[8] Bork quoted the Fifth Circuit Court of Appeals in *Cox*: "The prosecution of offenses against the United States is an executive function within the exclusive prerogative of the Attorney General.... The functions of prosecutor and judge are incompatible." Bork subsequently argued,

"Congress' duty under the Constitution is not to enforce the laws but to make them. The Federal courts' duty under the Constitution is not to enforce the laws but to decide cases and controversies brought under the laws. *The Executive alone has the duty and the power to enforce the laws by prosecutions brought before the courts.* To suppose that Congress can take that duty from the Executive and lodge it either in itself or the Courts is to suppose the Congress may by mere legislation alter the fundamental distribution of powers dictated by the Constitution.[9] (emphasis added)

The Department of Justice is the president's primary instrument for law enforcement, although he has additional institutional resources to use. The subordinate who heads the Justice Department is considered a member of the "inner cabinet" because of both the functional and political significance of his position. Cronin explains,

The Justice Department traditionally serves as the President's attorney and lawyer. This special obligation results in continually close professional relations between White House domestic policy lawyers and Justice Department lawyers. Few people realize that the White House is constantly dependent on Justice Department lawyers for counsel on civil rights developments, presidential veto procedures, tax prosecutions, anti-trust controversies, presidential pardons recommendations, regulatory agency oversight, and a continual overview of the congressional judiciary committees.[10]

The Criminal Division of the Justice Department, of course, has responsibility for all federal criminal prosecutions. In this area, ongoing consultation between Justice Department lawyers and White House staff would violate the essential premises upon which federal prosecutions are supposedly based. As Henry Petersen, head of the Criminal Division, advised presidential staffer James Dean, White House personnel should "not get involved in any way... with any criminal case."[11]

Any attorney general inevitably will experience some conflict between law and loyalty to his political chief. Victor S. Navasky wrote of the "tension between law and politics which is built into the Attorney General's office." He discussed two contrary images of the Attorney Generalship.

One emphasizes the legal and procedural obligations of the job. Abraham Lincoln's Attorney General, Edward Bates, described it when he observed, "The office I hold is not properly political, but strictly legal; and it is my duty, above all other ministers of state, to uphold the law and resist all encroachments, from whatever quarter, of mere will and power."

The other frankly recognizes that the Attorney General is the President's chief political officer and his main job is to execute the President's will. Attorney General Robert Jackson was acting in that tradition when he supported FDR's 1941 seizure of the North American Aviation Corporation.[12]

Later as an associate justice of the Supreme Court, Jackson acknowledged the political dimension in the 1941 "enforcement action." Responding to an attempt by Truman's solicitor general to use the incident as precedent in the *Steel Seizure* case, Justice Jackson said, "While it is not surprising that counsel should grasp support from such *unadjudicated* claims of power, a judge cannot accept self-serving press statements of the *attorney for one of the interested parties* as authority in answering a constitutional question, even if the advocate was himself. But prudence has counseled that actual reliance on such nebulous claims stop short of provoking a *judicial test*" (emphasis added).[13]

One of the reasons why contemporary observers of the criminal justice system are directing discussion and study to the issue of discretion is that, generally, police and prosecutorial discretion are not subject to judicial review. Similarly, presidential discretion is primarily subject only to inexact and delayed political review. Discretionary decisions by federal officials to prosecute or not to prosecute are in a sense less subject to popularly based political review than such decisions on the local level. This is due to greater centralization of the federal system under the president as *the* chief executive and the appointment of prosecutors by his authority. Davis comments,

When the prosecuting power is in an independent regulatory agency, no other officer of the government can review either a decision to prosecute or a decision not to prosecute. The White House has some control through the power of appointment and reappointment, but that control may be more likely to contribute to uneven enforcement than to relief from it. Congress in creating independent agencies probably lacks power to reduce the President's explicit constitutional power to "take Care that the Laws be faithfully executed," but *the President normally refrains from interfering with the prosecuting power of the independent agencies.* The practical fact is that that power, though enormous is unsupervised. A check by Congress or its committees is always a possibility, and the mere potentiality of such a check may have some effect, but legislative supervision of exercise of the prosecuting power is seldom, if ever, meaningful.[14] (emphasis added)

In relation to the Department of Justice's enforcement of law, Davis observes, "Judicial review of decisions to prosecute or not to prosecute is almost totally absent." He quotes an opinion of the Court of Appeals for the District of Columbia to illustrate:

Few subjects are less adapted to judicial review than the exercise by the Executive of his discretion in deciding when and whether to institute criminal proceedings, or what precise charge shall be made, or whether to dismiss a proceeding once brought. . . . While this discretion is subject to abuse or misuse just as is judicial discretion, deviations from his duty as an agent of the Executive are to be dealt with by his superiors. . . . *It is not the function of the judiciary to review the exercise of executive discretion* whether it be that of the President himself or those to whom he has delegated certain of his powers.[15] (emphasis added)

When acting Attorney General William Katzenbach directed a U.S. attorney not to sign a perjury indictment of two black witnesses, the district court, in the *Cox* case mentioned above, cited the U.S. attorney for contempt. The circuit court reversed, holding:

It follows, as an incident of the constitutional separation of powers, that the courts are not to interfere with the free exercise of the discretionary powers of the attorneys of the United States in their control over criminal prosecution.[16]

The broad scope of the president's discretion includes responsibility for appointment of subordinates and their direction and supervision. Executive responsibility for performance of subordinates has often been discussed, and the "misuse" of discretion by a presidential appointee is a political debit in the president's public account. The extent to which subordinates' wrongful action or bad judgment will actually hurt the president politically depends upon a host of factors. One is the chief executive's manner of handling the episode when it becomes a matter of public record.

Direct analysis of the president's role in the administration of criminal justice policy is particularly difficult because of federalism, the complexity of the policy process, the fragmentation of power in the implementation of policy, and the nature of the primary materials generated by those who make policy decisions in the day-to-day operation of government. Such materials are often "intra-office" or confidential. Generally they are beyond the reach of scholars, especially the papers of the presidential staff. There is a real need for more systematic study of the staff papers, which are or will be available at the presidential libraries. Such study would perhaps provide a data base that could greatly facilitate the analysis of the exercise of discretionary power in criminal justice policy.

In assessing existing research on the presidency, Hugh Heclo concluded, "only rarely has research . . . systematically delved into interactions between the Presidency and operational reality in the bureaucracy. A major exception to this generalization is in the area of defense and foreign policy. . . . But the fact remains that we know more about Presidents' social habits than about the underlying causes of the widely publicized charges of bureaucratic unresponsiveness to Presidential leadership, particularly in domestic policy issues."[17]

Despite present limits of research, considerable insight into the attitudes of presidents and their appointees relating to the bureaucratic reality of criminal justice can be derived from commentaries and recollections of highly visible presidential appointees.

As former Attorney General and Solicitor General Francis Biddle noted about his stint with "discretionary justice":

The work combines the best of private practice and of government service. He determines what cases to appeal, and the client has no say in the matter, he does what his lawyer tells him, the lawyer stands in his client's shoes, for the client is but an abstraction. *He is responsible neither to the man who appointed him nor to his immediate superior in the hierarchy of administration.* The total responsibility is his, and *his guide is only the ethic of his* own profession framed in the ambience of his experience and judgment. And he represents the most powerful client in the world.[18] (emphasis added)

Moreover, as attorney general, Biddle noted:

I had to learn by experience when and how far to oppose the President when he wanted to make a bad political appointment. There were times when one could insist on a better man: and he liked to have the satisfaction of supporting one, *not so much, I think, because he was concerned with putting men of professional competence* on the bench, but rather that, surrounded by the plaudits of the hungry office seekers who favored and flattered, and lay on the threshold of his door, he responded happily to the applause of those of his friends who really counted—Felix Frankfurter and Charles C. Burlingham and George W. Norris—men who were devoted to the necessity of the best, not only from the professional angle, but from the deeper consideration of a humane and broadly liberal approach to life, of which the law was so important an expression:[19] (emphasis added)

A president must often respond (or so it is perceived) to those who are not "devoted to the necessity of the best." The political and other pragmatic factors involved in presidential selection of judges were discussed by Victor Navasky. In explaining one instance when the Kennedy administration was able to secure the appointment of an able moderate to the Southern District Court of Florida, the author of *Kennedy Justice* stated:

That the Kennedys were able to outmaneuver the Florida Senators on this nomination is a tribute to their ingenuity and occasional expertise at dealing with the bureaucrats of judicial selection—deploying, as they did, the Senators and the ABA to the ultimate benefit of the judiciary. But then one must ask why they didn't use such tactics to thwart the nominations of the more obvious segregationists. *The answer is partly that they did not care enough in terms of other Presidential priorities to risk the political consequences,* but mostly it is to be found in the role played by the third major participant in the judicial selection process—the American Bar Association.[20] (emphasis added)

Navasky's study *Kennedy Justice* revealed another constraint on the implementation of presidential preferences in enforcement policy: that imposed by the resistance, or contrary preferences, of well-entrenched bureaucrats. John Edgar Hoover's initial recalcitrance in responding to the need for vigorous enforcement of civil rights in the South and his general official indifference to organized crime activities are examples.

Inevitably, the different orientation of those whose first duty is to serve the president and those who have responsibility for administering an ongoing policy will lead to some dissonance. The drama of Watergate and the resignation of President Nixon tended to obscure the fact that there normally is a kind of operational tension between the "president's people" and those who may also be his supporters but who are immediately concerned with policy implementation. Such tension touched deliberations within the Justice Department concerning the possible prosecution of Bert Lance. Such tension, if there is any element of accuracy in Jack Anderson's reporting, probably surrounded the issue of the disputed Kirbo-Vesco affair.

This discussion has indicated that the constitutional charge to the president to take care that the laws be faithfully executed assigns great discretion to the chief executive. The formal power to appoint officers who will administer criminal justice policy and the responsibility to direct them involve much discretionary judgment. Further, the inevitability that those the president appoints will also exercise discretion contributes to the totality of discretion for which the president is responsible. In the language of the introductory metaphor, the "trees" of appointment power and the subsequent discretion of subordinates contribute much to the depth—and sometimes the darkness—of the president's discretionary forest.

THE POWER TO PARDON

Much like the grant of discretion entailed in the "faithfully" execute the laws clause, the president is granted absolute discretion by the plenary pardon power assigned in Article II. As citizens were so vividly reminded by Gerald Ford's pardon of Richard Nixon, the president can pardon suspected criminals even before they have had a day in court. The pardon of Nixon helped to lower Ford's original Gallup approval rating from 71 percent to 50 percent during the first month of Ford's presidency.[21] Besides its devastating impact on the concept of justice and the idea that no one is above the law, the pardon indicated a good deal about Ford's concept of discretionary power.

Unlike other decisions, Ford apparently did not consult many advisors when he decided to pardon his predecessor. The decision was a personal one, developed in secrecy. Ford presumably change his mind about a pardon because he had told congressional confirmation committees earlier that "the American people would not stand for a pardon" and that he did not intend to grant one. In spite of relentless charges that Ford had pardoned Nixon as a quid pro quo, and despite the courageous questioning by Congresswoman Elizabeth Holtzman of New York, no evidence has been produced that would indicate Ford acted illegally, unethically, or unconstitutionally. The most important point about the Nixon pardon may be that within one month of assuming the presidency, Ford acted like three presidents before him. That is, on a major decision he closed the decision-making process to dissenters, secretly developed his own response, and then took unilateral, nonreciprocal, discretionary action without adequately assessing the costs of his action on the criminal justice system.[22]

In instances of "closed decisionmaking" in the realm of defense and national security, Ford and his predecessors could claim continuity with that mode of action by predecessors. However, in the matter of the pardon, Ford apparently ignored the established general procedures and standards for granting pardons.[23]

Presidents can, of course, pardon individuals and set certain conditions for the subject's behavior. In 1974 the Supreme Court ruled 6 to 3 in *Schick v. Reed* (419 US 256) that the president has the power to grant conditional pardons. The case involved a prisoner who was sentenced to death by court-martial, but in 1960 the president changed his sentence to life imprisonment on the condition that he would never be eligible for parole. When the Supreme Court invalidated the death penalty in *Furman v. Georgia* (408 US 238, 1972), the prisoner asked the Court to require the U.S. Board of

Parole to consider his application for parole. Chief Justice Warren Burger, writing for the majority, maintained:

At the time of the drafting of our Constitution it was considered elementary that the prerogative of the English crown could be exercised upon conditions.... A fair reading of the history of the English pardoning power, from which our Article II, Section 2, derives, of the language of that section itself, and of the unbroken practice since 1790 compels the conclusion that the power flows from the Constitution alone, not from any legislative enactments, and that it cannot be modified, abridged, or diminished by the Congress.... Considerations support an interpretation of that power so as to permit the attachment of any condition which does not otherwise offend the Constitution. The plain purpose of the broad power... was to allow plenary authority in the President to "forgive" the convicted person in part or entirely, to reduce a penalty in terms of a specified number of years, or to alter with conditions which are in themselves constitutionally unobjectionable.[24]

Thus, the pardon power is absolute, but the conditions of any pardon must not offend the Constitution. It is still an open question whether Ford's unconditional pardon of Nixon for all crimes that he committed or *may* have committed any time during his tenure as president offended the Constitution. Certainly the substance of Ford's pardon decision was violative of established norms and procedures.

Closely related to the pardon power debate is the president's discretionary action in using "executive clemency" and "amnesty." For example, in 1960 the Eisenhower Department of Justice under William Rogers withdrew an indictment against Jimmy Hoffa for mail fraud charges before the presidential election because Hoffa was supporting Nixon.[25] After Nixon's defeat by John Kennedy, the Justice Department reactivated the indictment against Hoffa. Later, the Nixon administration in the 1970s granted Hoffa clemency in exchange for his political support in the 1972 election but with conditions that he refrain from any organizing activity within the Teamsters.

More recently, both Gerald Ford and Jimmy Carter used discretionary power in creating their respective amnesty programs for draft resisters and deserters from the Indochina conflict. Carter was pressured by certain opinion leaders to grant some form of clemency to Patricia Hearst.

INFLUENCING CRIMINAL JUSTICE

The administration of justice in this country should, according to maxims of fundamental fairness, be divorced from partisan politics. Yet the vast amount of discretion the president has can allow a disproportionate partisan influence on the Justice Department's decisions to prosecute. The decision of whether to investigate largely determines the parameters within which discretion will be exercised. Henry Petersen, a career civil servant in the Justice Department for twenty years, said, "never, has an Attorney General that I know of, as long as I've been here, and that's quite a while now, reversed a major case after an investigation has begun and turned up evidence of a criminal violation."[26] The administration of justice can easily become politicized, given the practice of the president appointing campaign managers or old friends as attorney general.

Robert Kennedy was particularly sensitive to this as attorney general. Kennedy told a meeting of his staff on his first day in office "No politics, period."[27] Kennedy's administration of criminal justice confounded many experts in the field who had predicted that he would play partisan politics with justice. Two Democratic congressmen, three Democratic judges, five Democratic mayors, and numerous old-line politicians who had been close friends of Joseph Kennedy were indicted during the Kennedy years.[28] Kennedy once told his staff, "If you guys keep this up my brother is going to have to take me out of here and send me to the Supreme Court."[29]

If Robert Kennedy was relatively successful in leaving partisan politics out of the administration of justice, he was unable to keep presidential politics out completely. Even though he could be proud of the "significant actions" during his tenure as attorney general, including the drive against organized crime, the Hoffa conviction, the protection of freedom riders in the South, the moves for equal justice, the 1964 Civil Rights Act and the 1964 Criminal Justice Act, Kennedy was still amazed at the awesome potential for presidential interference and politicization of justice.[30]

During the steel price-hike battle of 1962, the Kennedy administration was particularly outraged at the inability of U.S. Steel and

Bethlehem Steel companies to hold the price line after workers had already agreed to a noninflationary pact. President Kennedy felt that he had been deceived by U.S. Steel President Roger Blough, and the attorney general's office asked the FBI to make a preliminary investigation of the possibility of a price-fixing violation of the antitrust laws. The FBI responded with unusual swiftness. Agents descended upon steel executives to interview them in their offices, and it also interviewed newspaperman who had been interviewing the businessmen. In short the Kennedys were prepared to play "hard ball" (in their terms) with the steel executives.[31]

When U.S. Steel backed down from the original price hike, the Kennedy administration, and especially the Justice Department, was sometimes criticized for the selective use of police force and arbitrary justice. Charles Reich, professor at Yale Law School, asked, "Are crimes by steel and other industries permitted so long as the criminals 'co-operate' with the administration?"[32]

Civil libertarians were critical of what was viewed as Robert Kennedy's strong-armed justice. Yet as Schlesinger noted, Kennedy really broke no law, did nothing that was unethical, and was true to the Constitution. It was simply a matter of "selective deployment of executive power."[33] As Robert Kennedy noted about the alarming prospect of so much discretionary power:

Yes, it is rather scary, there's no question about that; and it can be abused and misused. [The alternative] would have been bad for the country... and it would have been bad all around the world because it would have indicated that the country was run by a few manufacturers.... I agree it is a tough way to operate but under the circumstances we couldn't afford to lose it.[34]

The Nixon administration took the concept of a "potential" politicized justice system and changed it into an actual politicized justice system. Attorney General John Mitchell handed down a series of indictments against antiwar leaders and opponents of the Nixon administration on trumped-up conspiracy charges. Perhaps the trial that best illustrates Nixon's attempts to influence the outcome of justice was the conspiracy trail of Daniel Ellsberg and Anthony Russo. The Justice Department charged Ellsberg and Russo with violating three statutes in their handling of the Pentagon Papers, and a federal grand jury returned an indictment. Russo and Ellsberg were charged with

1. Conspiracy to defraud the United States of its lawful governmental function of controlling the dissemination of classified government studies, reports, memoranda, and communications
2. Violation of the Espionage Laws which make it a crime to retain or transfer the unauthorized persons material relating to the national defense
3. Stealing government property[35]

The euphemistically worded first charge, "conspiracy to defraud the United States of its lawful governmental function," was another way of saying that Ellsberg and Russo had challenged the discretionary powers of the presidential secrecy system. The second charge referred to "unauthorized persons" which presumably meant the press and the American people. In the third charge, the Justice Department apparently wanted to establish that information was property. Unfortunately, crucial questions posed by the charges against Ellsberg and Russo were never resolved in a court of law. Because of Nixon's overzealous attempts to influence the outcome of the trial, including offering the sitting judge a better judicial post, Judge Matthew Byrne finally dismissed the case. As Leonard Boudin noted, "So long as the law remains unclear in its defense of the individual's right to speak up, governments will likely be tempted to use concepts like 'theft of property' and 'espionage' to embrace communication of embarrassing information to the American people."[36]

SYMBOLIC LEADERSHIP IN THE CRIMINAL JUSTICE SYSTEM

Perhaps the most important source of discretionary power that the president has in the criminal justice arena is in symbolic leadership. Presidents are expected to send clear messages to citizens that "No person is above the law" and that "America is a *just* society." True, equality and justice are symbols and largely myths, but such myths serve as glue to hold the social fabric together. Presidents are important agents for the teaching of systems-maintenance myths.

Citizens expect lawful behavior from presidents and a commitment to equal justice in the land. When presidents deviate from the norm or send contradictory messages about the criminal justice system, such as "some citizens are above the law" and "America is not a just society," citizens experience dissonance. The function of White House leadership is to reinforce national confidence in the system of laws, not to contribute to its erosion.

President Nixon sent perhaps the most disjointed set of messages about criminal justice the nation has ever received from a national administration. As Paul McCloskey has observed,

It is incredible that a President who was himself a lawyer should nominate G. Harold Carswell, a self-proclaimed racist, to the Supreme Court, comment on the guilt of the accused (Charles Manson) before trial, interfere without legal authority in the appellate judicial process (Lieutenant Calley), and suggest "minimal compliance" with Supreme Court decisions he found it politically beneficial to disagree with (Swann). The law of the land demands his respect as much as it demands that of the people he governs.[37]

If Nixon's messages and symbolic acts indicated he had little respect for the judicial process, the ultimate message of his behavior in the Watergate coverup was that the president of the United States was beyond and above the law.

The Watergate investigations by the Ervin Committee, the Special Prosecutor, and the House Judiciary Committee brought to light numerous instances of executive lawbreaking. Arthur M. Schlesinger commented in *The Imperial Presidency*:

As for the President himself, he consistently denied that he had known either about the warfare of espionage and sabotage waged by his agents against his opponents or about the subsequent cover-up. If Nixon had known about these things, he had himself conspired against the basic processes of democracy. If he really had not known and for nine months had not bothered to find out, he was evidently an irresponsible and incompetent executive. For if he did not know, it could only be because he did not want to know. He had all the facilities in the world for discovering the facts. The courts and posterity would have to decide whether the *Spectator* of London was right in its harsh judgment that in two centuries American history had come full circle "from George Washington, who could not tell a lie, to Richard Nixon, who cannot tell the truth."[38]

The decision on Nixon's probity must await posterity's judgment. As discussed above, President Ford's proclamation pardoning Nixon in effect removed questions concerning degree of guilt from the courts. It is evident, however, that Nixon did participate in a wide range of highly questionable and probably illegal actions. Nixon predicted that his pattern of deception would be successful:

Bring it out and fight it and it'll be a bloody god-damned thing... rough as a cob... we'll survive.... Despite all the polls and the rest, I think there's still a hell of a lot of people out there, and from what I've seen they're— you know, they want to believe, that's the point, isn't it?[39]

Moreover, Nixon even believed that he had the power to order a breakin in the name of national security.[40] He even articulated the doctrine that presidential orders by their very nature can never be illegal in the name of national security.[41]

Presidential lawlessness vastly offends the Constitution, and it offends the criminal justice system when executive violators are not prosecuted and sentenced with the same vigor as "regular" criminals. When a vice-president is allowed to plead *nolo contendere* to charges that have been plea bargained, the Justice Department is sending messages that certain persons will receive preferential treatment when charged with crimes. Of course, this is not newsworthy to students of the criminal justice system who have long noted selective enforcement of the laws, as have the poor, blacks, and other minorities. Yet blatant messages of preferential treatment are contrary to society's expectation from symbolic leadership. The Justice Department under Nixon flagrantly violated the myth that no one, not even the president or the vice-president, is above the law.

During the "Year of Intelligence 1975–1976, the Church and the Pike committees investigated abuses by the intelligence agencies, and a new laundry list of executive lawlessness was revealed.[42] Former presidents may have been involved in assassination plots against foreign leaders. The CIA was engaged in contracting Sam Giancana and Johnny Roselli of the Mafia to conduct a "hit" on Fidel Castro. The FBI engaged in a COINTELPRO operation, which violated rights of Americans by infiltrating various groups in the guise of agent provocatuers. The FBI harassed, wiretapped, bugged, and engaged in a program of routinely opening mail of U.S. citizens. The FBI and CIA had used the tactic of illegal "black bag" jobs to gather information. The new revelations seemed never-ending.

The crucial point however, for the criminal justice system was that the officials themselves often engaged in illegal activities whenever necessity called. More importantly, once the political system found out about past wrongdoing, there was a conspicuous lack of prosecutions and convictions for intelligence agency illegalities. Again the message for the criminal justice system is that some citizens may break laws and be immune to prosecution by the Justice Department.

CONCLUSIONS

Though the president has formal powers (the power to appoint, the power to pardon, the constitutional obligation to see that the laws are "faithfully executed"), which in combination with his powers as national political leader create a vast area of discretionary power, the president's ability to direct criminal justice policy is limited by several factors. These include the geographic and demographic realities of our system—effective criminal justice policy depends upon many persons in many places. Another source of limitation on the president's capability to shape justice policy is the capacity and aspiration of the subordinates. Their zone of discretion is also great, and they serve in an environment in which they are particularly vulnerable to political influence. As the total political system's task is to find ways to hold the president accountable for his discretionary actions and decisions, so the president's central task is to devise means to direct subordinates toward the end of "law and right, justice and reasonableness" if those are his criminal justice goals.

We would suggest two practices which might be helpful in "controlling discretion" toward the end of de-politicizing justice. The president could require those who make recommendations on matters pertaining to the exercise of presidential discretion in criminal policy matters to prepare impact studies. These would be similar in purpose to those studies required by proponents of physical projects—the probable impact upon perceptions of, and practices in, the criminal justice system would have to be estimated by those recommending a particular use of discretion. Another possibility, also meant for intra-administration use, would be to require those subordinates who exercise discretion in terms of deciding whether to investigate or to prosecute to specify in writing the reasons for the decision reached. This would provide a means for monitoring discretion.

Certainly, one of the deeply felt needs of the people in 1976 was for a renewed trust in government, for a reaffirmation from national leadership that constitutional processes and the spirit of equal justice under law did in fact rule this society. That need can partially, perhaps, be met through judicious exercise of symbolic leadership, not just in the sense of a rhetorical war on crime in the streets or demands for more law and order, but in the sense of a meticulous concern for legality and proper procedure being reflected by the national administration.

Symbolism is of little effect, however, if it does not coincide with supportive, accepting attitudes in the people. The expectations of the people concerning standards of justice may go a long way toward shaping the "positive exercise" of presidential discretion in the criminal justice arena.

NOTES

1. Robert Dahl, *Modern Political Analysis* (New Haven, Conn.: Yale University Press, 1963).

2. Richard E. Neustadt, *Presidential Power* (New York: John Wiley, 1964).

3. Peter Sperlich, "Bargaining Overload," in Aaron Wildavsky, ed., *The Presidency* (Boston: Little, Brown, 1969), pp. 188–192.

4. Kenneth Culp Davis, *Discretionary Justice: A Preliminary Inquiry* (Baton Rouge: Louisiana State University Press, 1969), p. 4.

5. Thomas Cronin, "The War on Crime and Unsafe Streets, 1960–76: Policymaking for a Just and Safe Society," in *America in the Seventies*, ed. A. Sindler (Boston: Little, Brown, 1977), pp. 208–259.

6. Davis, *Discretionary Justice*, p. 3.

7. Arthur S. Miller, *Presidential Power* (St. Paul, Minn.: West Publishing Co., 1977), p. 105.

8. U.S. Senate, *Hearings Before the Committee on the Judiciary*, 93d Congress, "Special Prosecutor," part II, October 29, 1973 (Washington, D.C.: U.S. Government Printing Office, 1973), p. 451.

9. Ibid.

10. Thomas Cronin, "An Examination of White House-Departmental Relations," in *The Presidency in Contemporary Context*, ed. Norman C. Thomas (Boston: Little, Brown, 1975), p. 225.

11. John Dean, *Blind Ambition* (New York: Simon and Schuster, 1976), pp. 111–112.

12. Victor Navasky, *Kennedy Justice* (New York: Atheneum, 1971), p. 359.

13. Robert Jackson, concurring opinion in *Youngstown Sheet and Tube Co. v. Sawyer*, 343 US 579, 72 S.Ct. 863, 96L. Ed. 1153 (1952).

14. Davis, *Discretionary Justice*, pp. 208–209.

15. Ibid., p. 209.

16. *Hearings on Special Prosecutor*, p. 451.

17. Hugh Heclo, *Studying the Presidency*, a Report to the Ford Foundation, 1977, pp. 19–20.

18. Francis Biddle, *In Brief Authority* (Garden City, N.Y.: Doubleday, 1962), p. 97.

19. Ibid., p. 201.

20. Navasky, *Kennedy Justice*, p. 206.

21. "Gallup Poll," *Indianapolis Star*, January 16, 1977, Section 2, p. 16.

22. Jerald terHorst, *Gerald Ford and the Future of the Presidency* (New York: Joseph Okpaku Books, 1974), pp. 225–240.

23. See Miller, *Presidential Power*, pp. 94–95.

24. Edward J. Barrett, Jr., *Constitutional Law: Cases and Materials* University Casebook Series (Mineola, N.Y.: Foundation Press, 1977), p. 524.

25. Arthur Schlesinger, Jr., "The Pursuit of Justice: The Mob," in *Robert Kennedy and His Times* (New York: Houghton Mifflin, 1978), p. 291.

26. Dean, *Blind Ambition*, p. 111.

27. Ramsey Clark in Schlesinger, *Robert Kennedy and His Times*, p. 383.

28. Ibid., p. 398.

29. Ronald Goldfarb, "Politics at the Justice Department," in *Conspiracy: The Implications of the Harrisburg Trial for the Democratic Tradition*, ed. John C. Raines (New York: Harper and Row, 1974), pp. 119–120.

30. Robert Kennedy, *The Pursuit of Justice* (New York: Harper and Row 1964).

31. Schlesinger, *Robert Kennedy and His Times*, pp. 420–421.

32. Ibid., p. 423.

33. Ibid.

34. Cited by Schlesinger, *Robert Kennedy and His Times*, p. 424.

35. Leonard Boudin, "The Ellsberg Case: Citizen Disclosure," in *Secrecy and Foreign Policy*, ed. Thomas M. Franck and Edward Weisband (London: Oxford University Press, 1974), p. 292.

36. Arthur Schlesinger, Jr., *The Imperial Presidency* (Boston: Houghton Mifflin, 1973), p. 347.

37. Paul McCloskey, *Truth and Untruth: Political Deceit in America* (New York: Simon and Schuster, 1972), p. 11.

38. Schlesinger, *The Imperial Presidency*, p. 379.

39. *The White House Transcripts* (New York: New York Times-Bantam Books, 1974), p. 171.

40. U.S. Senate, John Ehrlichman, Testimony Before the Select Committee on Presidential Campaign Activities of the United States Senate: Watergate and Related Activities, 93d Congress, 1st Session, Book 6 (Washington, D.C.: U.S. Government Printing Office, 1973), pp. 2599–2601.

41. Richard Nixon to David Frost, interview text in *Indianapolis Star*, May 20, 1977, p. 12.

42. See the Church Committee Final Report, vols. 1 and 2 for the Select Committee to Study Governmental Operations with Respect to the Intelligence Activities of the United States Senate, 94th Congress, 1976; see also *The Village Voice*, "Pike Committee Report on Intelligence," February 16 and 23, 1976.

5

Celebrity Politics

The American political system has undergone a dramatic and radical transformation in recent years to become a new system of "celebrity politics." Andy Warhol may have uttered that famous populist sentiment that in the future everyone will be famous for fifteen minutes, but in reality, Warhol was wrong. Only celebrities are famous. The celebrity is celebrated, loved, admired, chronicled, watched, and sometimes hated. Celebrities rule American politics. There are just not enough ten-second sound bites to go around to make for a more democratic system. Neither can there be a philosopher-king in today's mediated political reality. There can only be the "celebrity-king" in this star-studded political system.

The celebrity politics system is characterized by (1) politicians who become celebrities, (2) celebrities who become politicians, (3) celebrities who become involved in political campaigns, and (4) celebrities who become involved in working for a political or social cause. This makes for a very entertaining show indeed.

The American political system has always had famous politicians, but the advent of television coverage in the 1950s made politicians reach the level of video stars. Before this time, citizens had known famous American celebrity-like politicians. George Washington was certainly the celebrated Revolutionary War leader, and Thomas Jefferson was a celebrated founding father of the Republic. Andrew Jackson was celebrated as an Indian killer, and famous generals like William Henry Harrison and Zachary Taylor garnered celebrity-like coverage. Abraham Lincoln became the celebrated martyred president, and U.S. Grant became the celebrated general of the Civil War. Teddy Roosevelt came from the celebrated Roosevelt family as did Franklin D. Roosevelt. John Q. Adams was a son of a former president, and Benjamin Harrison was celebrated for being a Harrison. Woodrow Wilson was the celebrated academician, and Dwight Eisenhower was the celebrated war hero and general of World War II. Yet none of these celebrities reached the television status that John F. Kennedy was able to achieve.

John Kennedy became the first televised celebrity president. Since Kennedy, the American political system has seen a proliferation of media-created political celebrities. The 1970s continued the trend of trivial celebrity politics by establishing "gossip" journalism of the Watergate investigative reporter mentality in political reporting. The 1980s finally gave us the institutionalization of the celebrity-star political system. Politicians became interchangeable with guest celebrities on television talk shows. They became the central players on the national news dramatic half-hour. They were overexposed in periodicals and newspapers. Citizens were reduced to watching politics rather than participating in the celebrity political system.

The next stage of the system evolved when celebrities from the entertainment field became politicians. First it was the California actors like Helen Douglas and George Murphy in the late 1940s and early 1950s. Then a grade B Hollywood actor and television pitch man named Ronald Reagan became governor of California in the 1960s, and American politics began to change fundamentally. A whole host of celebrity entertainers, sport figures, and celebrated heroes took the political scene. Former Buffalo Bills quarterback Jack Kemp became a member of the House of Representatives, and former New York Knicks basketball star Bill Bradley became a senator from New Jersey. Among the many examples of celebrity politics, John Glenn, the famous astronaut, became a U.S. senator; Clint Eastwood became mayor of Carmel, California, and Fred Grandy, "Gopher" from the television show "Love Boat," became a congressman from Iowa. P. T. Barnum may have warned us that a sucker is born every minute, but in the new televised celebrity star political system, it was possible to make millions and millions of U.S. citizens into suckers every second.

The celebrity political system continued to develop to encourage celebrities to endorse candidates and to raise money for them. Celebrity fundraising has been very important in every presidential election since 1972. This celebrity system came to be anchored by Hollywood electioneering from Ronald Reagan, Jane Fonda, Warren Beatty, Paul Newman, Joanne Woodward, Bob Hope, Sally Field, Jessica Lange, Mike Farrell, John Wayne, Ed Asner, Robert Redford, Barbara Streisand, and many others.

Then the late 1960s and particularly the 1980s saw the curious phenomenon of celebrities working on causes rather than tainted political candidates. Celebrities took part in the civil rights movement, the antiwar movement, the anti–nuclear power plant movement, the environment movement, the anti-nuclear weapons movement, the peace movement, the anti-aparteid movement, the anti–world hunger movement, the AIDS research movement, Amnesty International, and the Farm Aid movement among others. Hollywood supplied many of these celebrities in causes, but many came from dance, Broadway, sports, and especially rock music in the form of help from Bruce Springsteen, Jackson Browne, Bob Dylan, Bob Geldof, Harry Chapin, U–2, Tracy Chapman, Sting, Steve Stills, John Mellencamp, and many others.

Finally by the end of the 1980s citizens were reduced to watching the celebrity star political system as a sideshow. Citizens did not participate in politics but like Chance, the gardner in *Being There*, they "liked to watch." The media told celebrated political tales of Lee Iaccoca, Don Trump, Jerry Falwell, Oliver North, Henry Kissinger, Gerald Ford and Gerry Ferraro, Ed Koch, Dan Quayle, Gary Hart, Joe Biden, Douglas Ginzberg, and many others. The quality of political debate became trivialized. The gossip quotient increased. The entertainment increased. Political celebrities had "positives" and "negatives" in their people-meter quotients. Since citizens developed a two-day media attention span, no one remembered any historical context. Events appeared on the television screens like micro shooting stars vying for attention in a cosmic consciousness. The American political system of Washington and Lincoln had been transposed into the prime-time political news show. Politics lost salience, intensity, and meaning. Important domestic and international questions could no longer be differentiated in the bombardment of sound bites coming from mass media. It had become the great political coup in American political history. The democratic political system was overthrown not by some fascist generals or some Communist government's invasion, but rather by the celebrity political system. The change was swift and final. It did not cause much pain, and it was highly entertaining. The celebrity system helped citizens relieve themselves from a state of perpetual boredom. It was new age politics for citizens who had lost the ability to perceive the consequences of the star-studded celebrity political system.

DRAMATURGICAL CONTEXT

An approach to a behavioral framework to explain presidential action is the dramaturgical context. This view that human behavior can be understood as dramatic action has a long tradition dating back to ancient Greeks and in later years to William Shakespeare. Act II, Scene VII, of *As You Like It* detailed:

> All the world's a stage
> And all the men and women merely players;
> They have their exits and entrances;
> And one man in his time plays many parts.

More recently Erving Goffman in his *The Presentation of Self in Everyday Life* used the metaphor of theatrical performances to explain human behavior. Goffman understood human behavior and interaction as theater with roles, team of performers who cooperate to present to an audience a given definition of the situation by impression management, and the audience.[1] Goffman observed:

We often find a division into back region, where the performance of a routine is prepared, and front region where the performance is presented. Access to these regions is controlled in order to prevent the audience from seeing backstage and to prevent outsiders from coming into a performance that is not addressed to them. Among members of the team familiarity prevails, solidarity is likely to develop, and secrets that could give the show away are shared and kept.[2]

Dan Nimmo used this dramatistic perspective to explain the performances in the drama of politics.[3] Political performance is made up of act (or acts), actor, motive, role, scene, and vehicle for addressing an audience. Nimmo outlined his approach:

Dramatistic theory, then, conceives of the individual as a performer who manages impressions people have of him by playing various roles. . . . From the dramatistic perspective all of us are members of the cast. We are "on stage"; i.e., through motivated role performances we present images for audiences to observe, interpret, and respond to. Our performances take place in particular settings and we use several media and props to convey the impressions appropriate to our roles.[4]

Nimmo applied this framework to two presidential performances during the war in Indochina. He said that there were many ways to review Johnson's and Nixon's performances.

One could argue that both Johnson and Nixon were overly optimistic about the possibilities for peace during their campaigns in 1964 and 1968. One could argue that both candidates intentionally deceived the American people. Yet one might argue in a dramatistic view that neither Johnson nor Nixon could be charged with deliberate deceit, since the very *drama* of running for president constitutes a framework of popular expectations that a politician should have peaceful intentions. That is, the logic for dramatic performance for running for office is not the same as the logic for dramatic performance while being president.[5]

The Dramaturgical Context sees political performance as not being inherently deceitful or faked. Politics is not deception, and politicians are not confidence men. Motives are not good or bad, nor conscious or unconscious. Nimmo concluded:

This approach is merely a device to emphasize that *images* people have of politics, politicians, and the mass, are, in themselves, *actions* that establish the contours of leader-follower relationships; they are actions that stem from and determine motives. . . . But the subtleties of politics make it hard to be precise about who is on stage and who is in the audience.[6]

This Dramaturgical Context has its obvious magnetism and glamour. Yet as a framework for approaching presidential behavior, it has some deficiencies. By removing normative and descriptive judgments about motives of a performer, the drama critic is stripped of powerful reviewing tools. By allowing the performer great range in his role-playing over many different political settings, manipulation is removed from the play by definition. One can even carry the dramatic metaphors too far in analyzing political behavior. One knows when he is watching a play that it is only "make-believe"; therefore all political drama would be illusionary and deceptive. As a member of the audience, one can sense a rotten performance. Some actors do not play the part authentically. Some performers may deviate from the intent of the playwright. Some performers (i.e., presidents) may forget their lines, and some may become so wrapped up in their roles that they are always performing. Finally to carry this analogy to extremes to show some of the deficiencies of such an approach, many Broadway plays are so bad that they fold (i.e., Johnson and Nixon). The consequences of presidential behavior to the audience in terms of deprivations, unfulfilled needs, pain, and oppression are very real indeed.

The celebrity political system coincides with the dramatic rise of Madison Avenue advertising techniques of the 1950s. Advertising is the sign that indicates the rise of image posturing and the demise of political ideals. Advertising changed our basic concept of truth. It became standard operating procedure to shade the truth in order to promote a product. The great American advertiser learned how to make his advertisement newsworthy. P. T. Barnum, an early advertising pioneer and promoter of the nineteenth century, became a master at creating newsworthy media events. His success laid the groundwork for celebrity politics to develop in the twentieth century. Barnum had midgets, educated dogs, mermaids, "Swedish Nightingales," and a host of other exaggerations. He even became famous for making media events and other people famous. In the 1950s Madison Avenue took all that Barnum had used and then developed new techniques to convince people that they had to have a certain product. One of the products that came to be sold in American politics was the presidential image.

MEDIATED PRESIDENTIAL REALITY

As new means of communication become available in the political system, the ability of political bosses to monopolize the means of political communication diminished. The boss came to be replaced by the public relations expert in the manipulation of political communication. Moreover, the public relations expert soon became involved at the policymaking level. He acted to counter the power of the political bosses at the local levels within the party structures. The public relations technology and the expanding means of political communication have helped establish a star system in politics like the one in Hollywood. The public relations expert has helped to personalize the candidate in trivial ways. This trivialization of the presidency and of politics in general has created a condition that I call the "talk-show presidency." In the "talk-show presidency" presidential candidates and even presidents are presented to the electorate in such a way that they become personalities, celebrities, and television superstars. They seem like naturals on the cover of *Time* or *People*. Presidential candidates and presidents have also reached the stage in the development of American politics where they seem like natural and likely guests on talk shows, sandwiched between some actress promoting her movie and a stand-up comedian.

Today a candidate and a president must have high currency in his name recognition, have a public personality, and be adaptable. The growth of the advertising industry is the sign that indicates the rise of image thinking and the demise of ideals in our society. Advertising has reshaped our basic concept of truth with its pseudo-events and created news. The great American advertiser must know how to fashion the news and to make news. P. T. Barnum is still the model for the great promoter, advertiser, and public relations man. Barnum discovered how much the public really enjoyed being deceived.

Facts are no longer important, but making "facts" believable is the top art in our society. The illusion must be credible. Advertisers have given truth and experience new meanings. The public relations expert soon became involved in politics at the policymaking level. He acted to counter the power of bossism within the political party structures. The public relations expert appealed to a wider constituency to get support. Moreover, the public relations experts also injected issues into campaigns since they believed that issues, images and words were important determinants of electoral outcomes.

Public relations experts, media consultants, and technological advisors have come up with new and creative ways to project images for presidential candidates. Candidates try to project truthfulness, honesty, competency, credibility, composure, warmth, toughness against perceived enemies, compassion for underprivileged, and other presidential qualities. Media events help project certain qualities. In his classic work *The Image: A Guide to Pseudo-Events in America* Boorstin argued that Americans had a passion for pseudo-events, synthetic heroes, prefabricated tourist attractions, and homogenized interchangeable forms of art and literature.[7] He argued that American life had become a showcase for images and pseudo-events.[8]

The debates as pseudo-events were ambiguous to the underlying reality of the situation.[9] As Boorstin observed about the 1960 debates,

the drama of the situation was most specious, or at least had an extremely ambiguous relevance to the main (but forgotten) issue: which participant was better qualified for the Presidency. Of course, a man's ability, while standing under klieg lights, without notes, to answer in two and a half minutes a question kept secret until that moment, had only the most dubious relevance—if any at all—to his qualifications to make deliberate Presidential decisions on long-standing public questions after being instructed by corps of advisors.[10]

Even though the debates obviously did not stimulate the national electoral turnout new highs in participation, they did provide national political theater at the highest levels. They provided symbolic reassurances that the democratic rituals of the challenging party versus the incumbent party were still in order. Burdened by the inadequate format that presented the news reporter as star and provided for very little real debate and confrontation, the debaters were asked to demonstrate presidential communicative skills and the ability to answer rapid-fire queries. In terms of the establishment of a national agenda and the quality of presidential leadership, the pseudo-event did not provide any substantive directions.

The execution of the debates served to fulfill the self-fulfilling prophecy inherent in pseudo-events.[11] The debates were well advertised and discussed in advance by commentators, strategists, news magazines, newspapers, and the major networks. The media hype approached the level as that found in the advertising of a professional football championship. The massive amounts of post-coverage gave witness to the "importance" of the pseudo-event and stressed the "reality" of the happening. As Boorstin noted tongue-in-cheek:

Even if we cannot discuss intelligently the qualifications of the candidates or the complicated issues, we can at least judge the effectiveness of a television performance. How comforting to have some political matter we can grasp.[12]

POLITICAL SYMBOLS AND ELITE MANIPULATION

The literature on the use of symbols to convey political messages is vast. Dan Nimmo has suggested that there are essentially three views concerning the uses of political symbols and their effect on the mass. Nimmo wrote:

One [view] is that an image is something a politician, or his aides, creates, projects, and sells; if the image has no mass consumer appeal, the politician simply creates a new one. The other view posits that the mass mind is not so easily manipulated, that images of politics reside instead in the minds of people, and political leaders adapt to them—since "beauty is in the eye of the beholder." [Third view] Any image is complex and multi-faceted, but that image is a concept useful to students in organizing and synthesizing a great number of ideas about how people perceive not only public figures, but all types of political objects.[13]

The first view, symbols as tools for the elite to manipulate the mass, has received some attention. Harold Lasswell, a pioneer in this area as in so many other areas within the discipline, helped devise techniques like content analysis to analyze political communication, war propaganda, and party platforms, for example.[14] For Lasswell the key questions were "Who says what, how, to whom with what effect?"[15]

Lasswell best stated his position regarding symbolic manipulation when he wrote, "The fate of an elite is profoundly affected by the ways it manipulates the environment; that is to say, by the use of violence, goods, symbols, practices."[16] Symbolic manipulation to

Lasswell is just one method available to elites to manipulate the masses in the distribution of values: deference, income, safety. For Lasswell, symbols were the ideology of the established order. Elites used sanctioned gestures and words to elicit "blood, work, taxes, applause, from the masses."[17] Lasswell observed:

When we speak of the science of politics, we mean the science of power. Power is decision-making. A decision is a sanctioned choice, a choice which brings severe deprivations to bear against anyone who flouts it. Hence the language of politics is the language of power. It is the language of decision. It registers and modifies decisions. It is battle cry, verdict and sentence, statute, ordinance and rule, oath of office, controversial news, comment and debate.[18]

Political scientists Thomas Dye and Harmon Zeigler also represent Nimmo's first view tradition. They argue that (1) elections are primarily a symbolic exercise that helps tie the masses to the established order, (2) mass opinion is inconsistent, unguided by principle, unstable, and subject to change, and (3) available evidence suggests that elites influence the opinions of masses more than masses influence the opinion of elites, in other words, mass publics respond to political symbols manipulated by elites, not to facts or political principles.[19]

Perhaps Murray Edelman has best kept the early Lasswellian tradition going in contemporary political science, though Lasswell continued to be creative. In Edelman's classic *The Symbolic Uses of Politics* he notes how "condensation symbols" (which condense patriotic pride anxieties, remembrances of past victories or humiliations, promises of future greatness or some other reassurances into one symbolic event, sign or act) are used by elites to manipulate masses into a quiescent state.[20] For Edelman, organized groups get tangible benefit from the elite, but unorganized groups (mass) get symbolic rewards, or reassurances. In his later writings, Edelman continued his same theme:

Government affects behavior by shaping cognitions of large numbers of people in ambiguous situations. It helps create their beliefs about what is proper; their perceptions of what is fact, and their expectations of what is to come. In shaping of expectations of the future the cues from government often encounter few qualifying or competing cues from other sources; and this function of political activity is therefore an especially potent influence upon behavior.[21]

Edelman sees that "political actions chiefly arouse or satisfy people not by granting or withholding their stable substantive demands, but by changing the demands and the expectations."[22] Although it is not his chief concern, Edelman assumes "government officials and other elites make conscious efforts to manipulate mass opinion."[23]

For Edelman government actions and rhetoric are responsible for (1) generation of the perception of popular participation and influence in policymaking, (2) generation of the perception that particular groups are hostile and evil, (3) the generation of the perception that political leaders can cope and will cope in the public interest with issues that concern and baffle mass publics, (4) generation of perceptions that particular groups are friendly and benevolent, and (5) generation of perceptions that particular kinds of action are evil.[24] Edelman argued, "If the socialization researchers were socialized to raise questions about the influence upon cognitions of the government itself, their data would establish the conclusion that nongovernmental influences (family, school and peers) serve chiefly to reinforce governmental ones."[25]

In Nimmos' second view (that the mass mind is not so easily manipulated and leaders adopt followers' images) one might place the works of Donald Devine and Richard Hamilton. Devine in his *The Political Culture of the United States* argues for the existence of Lockean liberalism as the basic widespread consensus within the political culture of the system.[26] This "Lockean liberalism" helps to maintain the regime, to be sure, but Devine places a great deal of faith in the mass consensus. The mass is not manipulated; their values and perceptions of symbols must be conformed with by elite's values or the system will collapse. Thus although he admits the power of elites in certain areas, political culture appears to be mysteriously maintained by the mass. One assumes by his logic that the mass has the power, for without their broad consensus the regime would fall. He does not stress elites maintaining consensus within the mass, but rather the power of the mass to maintain regimes.

Richard Hamilton, although he is careful not to argue that no manipulation ever occurs, portrays the masses as those "in the working-class-lower-middle class majority [who] have a wide range of unfulfilled wants that have not been erased by shrewd manipulative efforts."[27] Clearly for Hamilton the masses are not easily duped no matter how hard certain elites may try on certain issues. Hamilton wrote,

There is some reason to doubt the adequacy of the calculating and manipulative imagery. There is a question to be raised as to the realism of elite or upper-class understandings. Because of their isolation and "exclusiveness," their knowledge of the society is limited and, consequently politics based on that knowledge prove, with some frequency, to be rather strikingly mistaken. The claims of the effectiveness of the means at their disposal also might better be considered as an open question. The number of failures of the manipulative attempts are impressive. Unfortunately, given the theoretical predisposition, it is the spectacular confirmation of the manipulation claim that is written about, discussed and remembered.[28]

Hamilton's research contends that the masses are concerned with economic liberalism issues, and this preoccupation anchors them in their orientations and outlooks. He argues that it is precisely this anchorage that works against manipulative efforts, "particularly against the attempts to distract through the use of the distant or alarmist concerns."[29]

Finally Nimmo notes that "image is complex and multifaceted." Even though he claims to stand apart from the other two traditions (elite manipulation versus mass control of symbols), Nimmo in his *Popular Images of Politics* comes down on the side that believes the public shapes the parameters in which the elite must act within by public opinion.[30] His assumption is similar to Richard Merelman's assumption in Merelman's critique of the neo-elitist position. Merelman argues that the assertion by neo-elitists who argue for "false consensus" created by the elite, is empirically unprovable.[31] He contends that government is an aid in getting things for both elite and mass. He gives credit to the non-elite initiators when they force an elite into using only one option, sanctions. For Merelman this shows the strength of initiators as well as strength in the elite, because initiators have the power to restrict elite's alternatives to only one.[32] However, taking Merelman's position to its logical extreme, one comes to a rather untenable claim. It is like saying, "The powerless are strong because they forced the powerful elite into using only one option, that of *crushing* them."

Roger Cobb and Charles Elder present their "agenda-building theory," which in some ways is similar to Nimmo's view in the power of mass culture to establish elite behavior parameters.[33] They identify two kinds of agendas. One is the "systemic agenda of controversy," which consists of the full range of issues or problem areas that are both salient to a political community and perceived as legitimate subjects of governmental concern. The second is the formal agenda, which is the institutional or governmental agenda. The process of an issue arriving on the formal agenda is much more rigorous than the process to bring an issue into the "systemic agenda of controversy." Any institutional agenda is restricted by political culture and the prevailing attitudes as to what makes up appropriate matters for governmental considerations.[34]

In Cobb and Elder's model, issues must first be defined along five baselines: the degree of specificity of the issue, the scope of social significance, the extent of temporal relevance, the degree of complexity and the degree of categorical precedence.[35] Through symbol use and interaction with mass media, the issue is expanded to relevant publics. Next the issue is pushed for consideration on the agenda of decision makers as the issue goes through a selected pattern of entrance access.[36]

The relevant political behavior that deals with political socialization, attitude consistency, nonattitude phenomena, awareness in the electorate, effects of television, voting behavior, attitude formation, public opinion, linkage and ideology, at times tries to assess the effects of elites on masses in behavioral terms, and in much of the socialization literature the focus is on the effects of family, school, and peers in passing along political culture.[37] The role that political elites play in transmitting cultural values and maintaining regime orientations has not been a major concern. Only Jack Dennis and David Easton consistently recognized the importance that socialization plays in support for the regime and for the system itself. They are concerned with the consequences and functions of political socialization in system maintenance.[38]

Most other researchers just assume the importance of political socialization without specifying their theoretical bent toward broader questions of elite-mass relations. The great body of political socialization studies deals mainly with children's and adolescents' political socialization. There has been little focus on political socialization as a continuing process or on adult political socialization. The effect of mass media as a political socialization agent is still an open question. Finally, the effects of the elite, more specifically the president of the United States as a political socializer, have largely been ignored. Fred Greenstein has talked about "the benevolent leader" image;[39] Alfred de Grazia has explored various myths of the president;[40] and Thomas Cronin compiled the images that make up the "textbook presidency," which shapes future generations' orientations toward the presidency.[41] But they have taken these images as a given fact, and for the most part they have not concerned themselves with how presidents create new myths, foster the old myths that fit their purposes, and generally use myth as a tool to gain support for specific public policies.

Finally, I want to postulate one key approach to a framework to understand presidential behavior. I call this approach the symbolic manipulation approach, and it can serve as one guide for the study of the presidency. This framework was developed from the interesting directions that Murray Edelman pointed out in regard to elite manipulation of mass through the use of political symbols. The framework owes a great intellectual debt to Peter Sperlich's analysis of the predominant presidential power model as advanced by Richard Neustadt. Using Edelman's cardinal points and Sperlich's criticisms of Neustadt's model, one is in a position to piece together a framework to understand presidential behavior that I call the "symbolic manipulation approach."

The major assumptions and components of the symbolic manipulation approach include the following:

1. A political symbol is viewed as a cue, codeword, password, or device to facilitate communication between president and other actors. Since meanings of symbols vary from receiver to receiver, political symbols may be used for clear, direct understandable communication or they may be used to obfuscate.

2. The target for the symbol selection may be the president's staff, the bureaucracy, Congress, Supreme Court, media, opinion leaders, specific attentive publics, or the mass, for example.

3. Symbolic manipulation by the president is

a. The conscious selection of political symbols calculatingly evoked to gain support for specific policies,

b. The conscious misrepresentation of the facts by symbols in order to lie, to deceive, and to make inaccurate statements,

c. The uncalculated selection of symbols by the president to communicate which gain more important and larger meanings because of the inherent mythical qualities of the presidency. The office of the presidency is a symbol of the nation, leadership, power, authority, and it is a reservoir of symbolic support that flows to the office regardless of who the incumbent is because of political socialization patterns of the system and out of the American culture, and

d. The intentional selection of symbols to enhance the already large uncalculated symbolic support for the myths of the presidency, to fuel the old myths, to create new ones and to carry on socialization.

4. Any one of the four kinds of presidential symbolic manipulation may be used to gain compliance in the president's efforts to exercise his seven types of power relationships:

a. Reward Power—B (target) accepts president's influence because president is able to manipulate B's attainment of positive values.

b. Coercive Power—B accepts president's influence because president is unable to manipulate B's attainment of negative values.

c. Guilt Power—B accepts president's influence because B feels guilty if he does not comply.

d. Referent Power—B accepts president's influence because he identifies with president through an admiring identification or through the loss of his ego to the president in a total charismatic relationship.

e. Legitimate Power—the power that stems from internalized values in which B feels that the president has the legitimate right to ask B to do something, and B complies because B feels that he has a duty and obligation to accept influence from the legal authority.

f. Expert Power—B accepts president's influence because he attributes knowledge and expertise to the president, and B wants to behave logically and rationally by accepting expert influence.

g. Affective Power—B accepts president's influence because B emotionally identifies with president's positions and because B genuinely *likes* the president.

5. The test of the success of each of the power relationships is whether B accepts president's influence and to what degree.

6. Most importantly, all images are mediated by the mass media. Presidents and presidential candidates do not have unilateral control over the kinds of images that are ultimately conveyed to the citizen.

The American public has been bombarded with many uses of political symbols to evoke policy supports, to lie, to gain unconscious support for presidents through the myth reservoir, and to enhance the myth. The symbolic manipulation approach has some attractive features to the study of presidential behavior. While recognizing that presidents do have to bargain along the lines of the Neustadian approach in many cases, the symbolic manipulation approach realizes that presidents gain compliance to their desires for reasons other than the fact that they are effective bargainers or commanders. Presidential power, then is not only the power to bargain, but it is the power to manipulate symbols in the president's exercise of his power relationships.

Even presidential advisors can become part of this celebrity political system by manipulating symbols and playing the role of "expert" for the media. Witness the remarkable examples of celebrity politics found in the cases of Dr. Henry Kissinger and his protégé Alexander Haig.

Kissinger viewed U.S. foreign policymaking and his particular role within the foreign policy arena as a game of chess. Kissinger felt that he was a grand master in this game and he often used this chess analogy to explain foreign policy performances to the public. Kissinger, however, could not stand dissent or criticisms of his policies. As he explained, in effect, kibitzers are not allowed in a championship chess match, and in the same fashion, Kissinger did not tolerate kibitzers.

Yet Kissinger overlooked many important facts with respect to his chess analogy. Although international diplomacy, like chess, requires strong strategic capabilities, gamesmanship, and mental prowess, the stakes in international diplomacy are very real indeed in terms of human values, suffering, life, and death while chess is, after all, only a game. The conduct of chess may require no kibitzers, but the conduct of U.S. foreign policy demands opposing viewpoints, alternatives, and criticisms. Finally, Henry Kissinger was no Bobby Fisher.

Kissinger showed great ability to disassociate himself from the various scandals that later hit the Nixon administration. Kissinger was able to convince others that he was not involved in any corrupt acts of state while the rest of the Nixon administration principals suffered public reprobation. Indeed, fifty-two senators led by Alabama Senator James Allen passed a resolution in 1974 that stated Kissinger's "integrity and veracity are above reproach." This was passed before the Senate Foreign Relations Committee could even begin an investigation of Kissinger's role in the illegal security taps.

Kissinger had always been popular with the press. He seemed to be one of the few bright spots within a dull, lackluster, corrupt administration. He got incredible national press as "the White House swinger with Hollywood starlets," "the man behind detente with Soviet Union," "the architect of the new relations with the People's Republic of China," "the man who ended our involvement in Indochina," "Super K," "Chief Diplomat," "Mideast peacemaker," and "America's Metternich."

For political scientists Kissinger's case was peculiarly attractive. He was, after all, an academician from Harvard in the field of international relations, who had the chance to become a practitioner as assistant for national security affairs to President Nixon in 1969. Some criticism of Kissinger naturally reflected jealousy over his diplomatic and media successes by members of his discipline. Kissinger had made a remarkable climb from professor to international legend in a few short years.

But most of the criticism of Kissinger's policy grew out of his inconsistencies and contradictions. His conduct in the Vietnam disengagement was controversial. He promised "peace was at hand" a week before a U.S. presidential election; yet, he was the guiding force in the resumption of the terror bombings of Hanoi during Christmas 1972. His Vietnam War record and conduct prompted his severest critics to label him as one of the great mass murderers of the twentieth century.

Nixon and Kissinger were skilled at staging international foreign policy pseudo-events. For example the "Nixonger" policies with the diplomatic breakthrough with the People's Republic of China became a carefully staged media event for U.S. television to cover. Some top diplomatic correspondents came to believe that Kissinger was their friend and more important that when he gave information out on background, the information was correct. One example of correspondents who were on the information pipeline as fed by Henry Kissinger were the respected Martin and Bernard Kalb brothers.

Kalb and Kalb have revealed their view of the story in *Kissinger*, which follows the secretary of state from the early days of childhood to Watergate. Kissinger's diplomatic strategies and tactics are seen in the Kalbs' treatment of his years before power, SALT and detente with Russia, the China breakthrough, Vietnam negotiations, Mideast crisis, and Watergate's impact on foreign policy.[42] The book was quite revealing in the area of Kissinger's personality and its effect on U.S. foreign policy. But it is obvious that Kalb and Kalb's close contact with Kissinger as diplomatic correspondents has been conducive to their being overcharmed by the man they call "Henry." The Kalb brothers are fairly in awe of Henry Kissinger, and their book reflects it.

Kissinger's secretive "Lone Ranger" style of diplomacy became a campaign issue in 1976 as it was attacked by candidates Jimmy Carter and Ronald Reagan. Yet when Kissinger left the office of secretary of state, he had higher levels of performance approval than any of his critics. He obviously had scored enough symbolic successes and staged enough pseudo-events to be well regarded by important opinion leaders. His appearance on the Georgetown cocktail circuit also provided many lines of favorable press.

Through various public relations techniques like publicity, secrecy, deception, partial stories, selective leaking and historical revisionism, Nixon and Kissinger were able to count as successes the diplomatic breakthrough with the People's Republic of China, Kissinger's Mideast diplomacy, detente with the Soviet Union, ending U.S. military involvement in Indochina, and destabilization of the Allende regime in Chile.[43] Unfortunately, many people suffered throughout 1969 and 1974 while Nixon and Kissinger played their game of international chess. Although it has been labeled as Nixon's strong point, his foreign policy decision making lacked conscience, honor, and principles. Moreover, the foreign policy of Nixon and Kissinger was incoherent, elitist, costly, and vastly overrated. Only through symbolic deception was the Nixon administration able to sell what were essentially foreign policy tragedies like Vietnam, Cambodia, and Chile as victories.

Alexander Haig and his Career Advancement

Kissinger's protégé Alexander Haig had particular skill at being involved in questionable activities during the Nixon administration and resolving his participation in these activities by claiming that he was not in a policy-making position and that he was just following orders. At Haig's confirmation hearings in January 1981, he was able to convince senators that he was just doing his job. Although he was overwhelmingly approved to be President Ronald Reagan's secretary of state, his unyielding devotion to loyalty still raised crucial questions about his ability to serve.

Consider some of the following nuggets from Haig's previous tenure as a loyalty-to-loyalty devotee. In 1969 as a deputy to Henry Kissinger on the National Security Council Haig delivered to the FBI the names of the people whom Nixon and Kissinger wanted to wiretap illegally including members of the National Security Council, government officials, and reporters from CBS News and the *New York Times*. Moreover, Haig researched the "raw files," that is, the transcripts and records of the wiretapping. There is no evidence available in the public record to suggest that Haig once said, "Mr. President or Mr. Kissinger, this is illegal and unethical, and I will not do this." Haig followed orders.

In 1970 Haig knew of the CIA's "Track II" plan, which was an attempt to assassinate Chilean General Rene Schneider in order to clear the way for a coup against Chilean President Salvador Allende. There is no evidence existing that shows Haig saying, "Mr. President, it is wrong to try to overthrow foreign regimes by force and subversion" or "Mr. President, it is morally wrong to engage in assassination plots against foreign government officials." Haig followed orders and kept quiet.

From 1969 to 1970 Haig was aware of the so-called "secret bombing" of Cambodia where Nixon and Kissinger arranged for the military to bomb a neutral country secretly in an effort that widened the war in Indochina. The bombing was kept secret from Congress, the media, and the American people so that the Nixon administration would not suffer any public reprobation. No evidence exists in the public record to show that Al Haig ever said, "You know, Mr. President, secret bombings of countries are unconstitutional. I do not think we ought to be doing these kinds of things, sir." Again Haig followed orders and remained loyal to loyalty.

In 1972 when Richard Nixon resumed the so-called "Christmas bombings of Hanoi" in the Indochina War to bring North Vietnam to its "knees," Al Haig did not counsel the president to resist the temptation to become the aggressor. On the contrary, Haig was one of the strong advocates of the plan. Haig was, once again, just following orders.

In 1973 as Nixon's White House Chief of Staff during the so-called "Saturday Night Massacre," it was Al Haig who relayed the messages to William Ruckelshaus (the new attorney general who had just replaced Elliot Richardson, who had resigned in protest over the first order) that he would have to fire special Watergate prosecutor Archibald Cox because Cox was seeking to gain access to the Nixon White House tapes in his investigation of Watergate. When Ruckelshaus refused the order from Haig, he was fired. There is no evidence to suggest that Haig felt his superior, Richard Nixon was in the wrong. On the contrary, Haig felt Richardson and Ruckelshaus were being disloyal. Haig stayed on and supported the president's decision.

On one White House tape, June 4, 1973, Haig is heard counseling the President to say, "You just can't recall," when asked about certain charges. Nowhere in the public record does Haig tell Nixon that "you must tell the whole truth about your involvement, and you cannot engage in any illegal coverups." Haig continued his pattern of loyalty to loyalty.

During the final days of the Nixon administration, it was Haig who first approached Gerald Ford to give him possible scenarios as to how the Watergate crisis would end. One scenario presented to then Vice-President Ford was for Nixon to resign and for the new president to pardon the former president. Haig was still remaining loyal to his commander-in-chief.

Finally in 1974 as White House chief of staff, Haig helped supervise the massive efforts by the Nixon administration to edit the White House tapes into the president's version. This version was released in April, and the Nixon administration's version of the White House tapes significantly differed from the actual transcripts of the White House tapes as reported by the House Judiciary Committee.

In all these matters it is clear that Alexander Haig technically did not break any laws. He did not, according to the Special Watergate Prosecutor Leon Jaworski, engage in any criminal activity. Yet it is also clear that Haig did not engage in any critical or ethical thinking during his years of public service 1969 to 1974. Haig was the typical foot soldier. He always followed orders. He was always loyal to his chief. Finally, Haig was always loyal to the idea of loyalty. He never questioned his orders.

As Haig so eloquently stated during his confirmation hearings, "No person has a monopoly on virtue, not even you, Senator." Yet the U.S. Senate almost systematically overlooked Haig's loyalty to loyalty. In effect, by confirming Haig, the Senate was telling other public servants that it is okay to wiretap your friends, use secret force and coercion to get what you want, attempt to assassinate people, subvert criminal investigations, use quid pro quo in making secret transactions, and be loyal to orders from superiors even if those orders might be unethical. The Senate was saying actually even more that it is okay to be associated with these kinds of events; the Senate confirmed that one might even get promoted in spite of them. In short, the U.S. Senate overwhelmingly confirmed, "loyalty to loyalty" by confirming Haig to be secretary of state.

Both Kissinger and Haig thrived in the star-studded celebrity political system by being friends of the media and providing some of the major leaks of our time. These close relations with members of the media who covered national security matters allowed Kissinger and Haig to emerge as insider political celebrities and experts without ever having to account for the consequences of some of their political decisions.

PRESIDENTIAL SYMBOLIC MANIPULATION

To most observers of the American political process, there is a contradiction between the claims by campaign managers and consultants, and the voters themselves over the impact of campaign events. Campaigners and their candidates tend to overestimate the public's interest in and potential for political participation and believe a well-run campaign can successfully convert, mobilize, and solidify voter preferences.[44] Voters, however, rarely acknowledge influences like campaign pledges and political advertising as important reasons for their candidate preference.[45] Indeed, there is evidence suggesting that candidate preference switching in the post-convention period is minimal.[46]

This contradiction between campaign managers' explanations and voters' explanations of candidate switching is mirrored, to some extent, in the voting literature. Contradictions can be found in the literature when one attempts to sort out the relative importance of *long-term* political predispositions (including socioeconomic characteristics, direction and strength of partisanship, and general issue orientations) and short-term, campaign-specific stimuli, that is, candidate image, campaign issues, and campaign events.[47] In elections marked by high levels of candidate conflict, emotional issues and frequent peaks of campaign drama, the political attitudes formed in the campaign often yield outcomes unrepresentative of the long-term predispositions in the electorate. For "normal" campaign periods, the most important role of the campaign is the way it "links" long-term predispositions to campaign-specific phenomena.[48]

Regardless of the temper of the electoral conflict, campaign periods can be thought of in terms of their purposive structuring and presentation of political phenomena. Political stimuli introduced by candidates during the election period are designed to advance their political fortunes. This holds true for both normal and abnormal electoral periods, although the conversion or reinforcement effect of the political communication may be unintended.[49] What remains stable across election campaigns is the degree certain types of political stimuli can be structured or controlled by the campaigner. Robert Agranoff suggests there are two types of messages the campaigner uses to structure his/her purposive media communication.[50] *Controlled messages* include activities such as "personal campaigning by the candidate and campaigner, party organization efforts, whether they be through mass media or delivered on a smaller scale."[51] The notion of control, then, comes from the capability of the campaigner to structure both the *content* of the message as well as the environment in which the message is communicated.[52] *Uncontrolled* messages are those messages that are transmitted by an uncontrolled communications channel. The major broadcast networks' coverage afforded to the campaign is an obvious example of an uncontrolled message.

The two classifications describe only the polar end points of a wide spectrum of message transmission control by the candidates. As Agranoff points out:

It becomes readily clear that not all uncontrolled media are completely uncontrollable, when one stimulates or attempts to structure media. Some would say that these are semi-controlled media messages. However, all uncontrolled media messages are qualitatively different from messages produced and placed by the candidate, not only because what is said is not controlled, but because the format through which it is delivered is considered to be *neutral and authoritative*, and is regarded by the audience as *information rather than propaganda*.[53] (emphasis added)

Any problems that campaigners face with the success of their controlled purposive communication can be surmounted by the judicious use of semi-controlled communications.[54] The main goal of such efforts is to use the "uncontrolled" environment of the media election coverage as a conduit for structured purposive communication. In other words, the goal is to create media events, or "pseudo-events," which are transmitted to the voters as straight political information, or "news."[55] As Doris Graber described the phenomenon:

At times, public meetings are arranged or conducted primarily for the propaganda value in swaying external audiences. As in public pageants, speakers unfold carefully prepared scenarios before audiences who presumably are dazzled by the status of the actors and the solemnity of the setting.[56]

At the most basic level, the debates were media events that the candidates entered in order to sell an image. The content of the debates was transmitted as a special form of persuasive political communication—the semi-controlled political advertisement. The debates were quintessential "pseudo-events" in Boorstin's terminology.[57] Debates, of course, were not spontaneous occurrences. The debates were carefully planned events that both candidates felt would fit in their electoral strategies. Participation in the debate was agreed to by the candidates primarily for the purpose of being reported, reproduced, and exposed to the massive audiences. For the candidates, the *coverage* of the event, rather than the event itself, assumed the greatest importance.

The candidates exercised a high degree of control over the event and its transmission. Both candidates, ironically, trained, studied, prepared, and practiced in order to appear spontaneous.[58] This *planned spontaneity* is one of the hallmarks of Boorstin's "pseudo-event." The success of the event in the eyes of the candidate (if he performs "well") as well as the media is measured by Nielsen Ratings. If the debates had the same national audience that a normal extended paid political advertisement receives, they would probably be considered failures. Fortunately for the candidates, the debates were considered as "news" and not as semi-controlled purposive communication and advertising. This notion might explain the large national audiences that the media events drew.

Yet these planned media events ("pseudo-events") should not be considered as imaginary or unreal events.[59] Once a "pseudo-event" occurs, regardless of the fact that it was contrived and staged, it becomes a real *political* event.

In sum, the debates offered the candidates a forum to present a ninety-minute political advertisement for their candidacy in the guise of a straightforward "news" or news-conference type of show. The only parts of the event and transmission that the candidate did not control were what questions would be asked and what the other candidate would say. Although the health of the democratic order would not be seriously imperiled if future debates of similar form and substance never materialized, the labeling of the debates as staged media events should not be taken to imply the debates lacked political impact.

The impact of televised purposive communications (regardless of the degree of control present) upon political attitudes and behavior is an area of strong controversy in the communications research literature. While few writers have totally accepted the theory that media exposure determines the content and scope of political beliefs and attitudes (often referred to as the "hypodermic" effect hypothesis) or dismissed the question of media effects entirely, disagreement exists as to the *degree* to which media transmissions affect political behavior.[60] At the core of this debate is the question as to whether media effects take the form of *crystallizing* or *realigning* previous political orientations by the provisions of "new" information or, rather, that information supplied by the media *reinforce* or validate earlier beliefs.[61]

The reinforcing hypothesis draws its support from the work done in the areas of selective perception and selective exposure.[62] The main idea is that individuals will seek out information that conforms to their own orientations and, when confronted with information which runs counter to their views, ignore dissonant transmissions. As Maxwell McCombs pointed out;

Implicit in these concepts of selective exposure and and perception is the idea of motivation, that voters are actively *motivated* to attend to supportive messages. Conversely, this view suggests that voters are also motivated to avoid contradictory, non-supportive political messages.[63]

While several studies have pointed out problems with this approach,[64] the overwhelming majority of the research on the effects of the 1960 presidential debates concludes that citizen evaluations of each candidate's debate "performance" were extensions of predebate attitudes toward both candidates and political parties.[65] One study on the 1976 presidential debates has shown that an individual's evaluation of a candidate's debate performance was strongly linked to predebate evaluation of the candidate's personal image and party.[66] There seems, then, to be some empirical evidence to suggest that the majority of voters evaluate campaign stimuli, such as the debates, in reference to prestimulus political predispositions. The implication is, as Patterson and McClure suggest, that the effect of political purposive communication is not as subconsciously subversive as many writers would have us believe.[67]

While most debate "effect" studies found that the debates reinforced the political predispositions of most respondents, the same studies indicated that a minority of the voters underwent shifts in candidate evaluation and support and for some, the change was associated with evaluation of candidate debate performance. While the actual size of this group can only be roughly estimated, even the most conservative size estimate of this "debate-switcher" group raises the possibility that the debate event may have had an important impact on the close elections of 1960 and 1980.

People who change their candidate preferences, or who change the intensity of that preference, over the course of the campaign period have been a source of constant interest to researchers ever since *The People's Choice*.[68] That work found significant differences between those voters who had constant preferences across the campaign period and those whose preference shifted during the campaign. The "constants" were more self-assured, more cooperative, better integrated into their communities, and broader in their interests with greater enthusiasm for the political campaign than the "changers." The "changers" had a limited range of community contacts and tended not to be associated with any formal or informal social or political groups. Recent research has observed that those voters most susceptible to political persuasion, and hence most likely to change their allegiances during the campaign, are more likely to be "detached" from the socio-political system and group memberships.[69] Terming this group "rootless voters" Edelman states,

One of the most confident conclusions we can reach from the communication experiments and electoral studies is that people without enduring commitments are the most susceptible to persuasion, both by means of mass communications and by personal influence.[70]

As Edelman contends, people who are removed from the reinforcing influence of social and political group involvement as well as the opportunity for information exchange that accompanies it are more susceptible to persuasion. We should expect these individuals to be more strongly affected by the staged drama of the media event than those who have a broader context with which to evaluate the event.

The "rootless voter" hypothesis, then, creates a set of expectations relating to the characteristics of those individuals who would be more likely to be influenced by events such as the presidential debates. First, those groups that tend to be organizationally inactive due to constraints related to membership access, time, or financial hardships should be more susceptible to political persuasion than those groups whose socioeconomic status allows greater opportunities for reinforcement of political orientation.[71] We should expect to see discrimination of persuasion effects along education, age, and income dimensions. Second, as Edelman notes, strong social and political ties influence the degree of persuasibility.[72] Given that the psychological involvement and motivation engendered by an individual's partisan identification remains the strongest and most durable form of political attachment, we should expect an inverse relationship between the degree of partisan commitment and the degree of persuasibility. Lastly, indications of "rootlessness" should be apparent in the individual's involvement in the campaign and in his/her differentiation of campaign-specific phenomena. Being more isolated from an environment that encourages information transmission and mutual reinforcement, those individuals who are less participant (in both an overt and psychological sense) and who have a less differentiated conceptualization of the candidates and issues involved in the campaign, are more susceptible to political persuasion.

The most attractive aspect involved with the "rootlessness' thesis is that it posits a model of attitudinal instability that is not based upon assumptions relating to respondent instability or an inability to conceptualize political phenomena adequately. Additionally this thesis does not argue that instability is the result of psychological alienation or system disaffect. It argues that those individuals who occupy relatively isolated positions in the social nexus are more greatly influenced by information transmissions (or transmissions that give the appearance of transmitting information) that encourage easy access and contain elements of high drama and importance. Changes in orientations brought on by such events may be better viewed as indications of a more direct and simplified form of political learning which occurs during the campaign period.

RONALD REAGAN: MASTER CELEBRITY COMMUNICATOR

The person who most benefited from this celebrity political system of the 1980s was Ronald Reagan. He was an outstanding personality, and this helped him emerge as an even more powerful celebrity after his rounds of debates in 1980 and 1984. Reagan's celebrity status and his high "positives" made it very difficult for the media to hold Reagan accountable for his actions.

Perhaps the most blatant attempt by the Reagan administration to keep information from the American public was the successful effort to keep the American media from covering the initial stages of the invasion of Grenada. Clearly the administration excluded the press, not for security reasons related to the operation, but foremost to keep the American people in doubt as to the nature of the operation.[73]

In the pre-Irangate Reagan presidency, the emphasis was on the control of information. All presidents to some extent try to monopolize state secrets. Information is power, and presidents like to be able to control as many actors in the political system as possible. Yet compared to modern presidents, when placed on a secrecy publicity continuum, the Reagan administration ranks with the Nixon administration for a penchant towards secrecy.[74]

A president may be prone to verbal gaffes and not be a systematic liar. For example, former President Gerald Ford often confused Ohio and Iowa, but no one thought Ford was intentionally shading the truth. When Reagan systematically exaggerated the situation for his own partisan version of reality, he became known as the "Great Communicator" rather than the "Great Distorter."

Among Reagan's more blatant lies included his efforts to dismantle the Voting Rights Act Extension of 1982 while taking credit for the passage of the bill after Congress approved it overwhelmingly. In 1980 Reagan promised to balance the federal budget much as candidate Jimmy Carter had done in 1976. Unlike Carter who admitted that he would be unable to balance the budget before his term ended, Reagan clearly had no intention at all of trying to cut federal spending. He sold himself as a fiscal conservative at the same time he embarked on the most massive federal defense expenditure in American history.

In 1983 the Reagan administration asserted the right to overthrow the regime in Grenada in order to protect American students who "might" be held hostage. It was meant to be the first preemptive hostage rescue in that it would save "hostages" before they were ever taken. Then the administration successfully sold the idea to most Americans that the invasion was necessary to stop a "Cuban colony." To sell this idea, the Reagan administration had to inflate Cuban military strength on the island. The administration claimed that Grenada had become a "terrorist training base," yet no evidence was ever produced to show that this was the case. The Reagan administration failed to report that a navy plane accidentally hit a civilian mental hospital and killed at least seventeen people. The administration claimed there were at least 1,100 trained Cuban soldiers on the island who had been "impersonating construction workers."[75] When the facts finally came out, the Pentagon later conceded that there were actually about 100 "combatants." The administration claimed that the invasion of Grenada had nothing to do with a public relations effort to take the pressure off the President for the ill-fated deaths of 243 marines in a terrorist attack in Lebanon.

ISOLATION AND TRAPPINGS

An imperial president is often isolated and has to deal with the extraordinary psychological impact that the trappings of the office can have on the incumbent. No one has made this case better than the late William Mullen in his chapter "Elevation and Isolation in the White House."[76] Certainly the Reagan presidency continued a trend toward isolated "sun king" presidents. Gerald Ford and Jimmy Carter both made conscious efforts to be "open presidents" who could not be accused of being isolated or enamored with the trappings of office. The Reagan presidency made a conscious choice to increase the isolation of the president and to take full advantage of the symbolic rewards that the trappings of power had to offer.

The legendary secluded vacations at the ranch, the "Troika," and Donald Regan's performance as White House chief of staff acted to isolate Reagan. The press found it difficult to track down their president for questioning. Secret Service security precautions increased so much after the 1981 assassination attempt on the president, that some charged the Secret Service with overzealous protection measures to isolate their president from the public. In 1984, the Secret Service carefully policed Reagan campaign rallies in a manner that hid dissent, forced critics to destroy anti-Reagan signs, and grouped protestors far away from the president.

There are whole groups of Americans who never appear in Reagan's isolated version of American reality. Reagan did not meet with poor people, feminists, the homeless, anti-nuclear activists, environmentalists, public interest groups, gay people, Native Americans, Asian immigrants, and a host of other Americans. The Reagan administration had reinstituted the "black-tie" presidency. He cavorted with millionaire friends at all-celebrity dinners. His wife Nancy was said to have brought back elegance and style to First Family living as opposed to the populist years of Betty Ford and Rosalyn Carter. The celebrity trappings of Reagan's life-style easily qualified for a mythical segment in popular culture consciousness of "The Lifestyles of the Rich and Famous." For despite Reagan's attempts to portray the image of the common-man presidential myth, Reagan clearly was one of the richest presidents ever to serve, and he acted like it.

MEDIA MANIPULATION

The administration that most often tried to manipulate the settings for public presidential appearances was the Reagan administration, which tried to maximize the numbers of live televised presidential appearances to go directly to the "American people" with scripted, rehearsed addresses. His advisors tried to minimize the number of presidential press conferences where Reagan would be called upon to account for his actions and his decision making. Both strategies were successful. Reagan relied on the televised address more than other presidents, and he had the fewest press conferences per year since live televised press conferences began. Reagan averaged 6.5 press conferences per year, and the closest president to Reagan in terms of hiding from the press is Richard Nixon with 6.6 press conferences per year.[77] Kennedy (22.6), Johnson (26.1), Ford (16.1), and Carter (14.7) all had more significant interaction with the press in the form of press conferences.

Not only was Reagan available for a minimum number of press conference exchanges, but his staff also cut off access to the president for off-the-cuff exchanges. Reporters were secluded behind ropes at strategic positions to limit access. Questions at photo opportunity sessions were eliminated. White House Press Secretary Larry Speakes became the *voice* of the Reagan administration to a higher degree than any other press secretary since the days of Ron Zeigler and the Watergate period.[78]

Reagan engaged in symbolic manipulation to degrees that seemed impossible before his presidency. He gave America heroes every time he spoke. He had heroes in the balcony when he gave his State of the Union addresses. He quoted Clint Eastwood "one-liners" that showed up as ten-second sound bites on the national news. He effectively used the 1984 Olympics, Rambo, Bruce Springsteen, and 1986 Statue of Liberty mythology for his own partisan political purposes. When one of his pet projects to prove that space shuttle flight is so safe and routine that the average American (Christa McAuliffe) could fly dramatically failed, he helped start the process that turned the crew into national heroes who were space "explorers." He celebrated the one-year anniversary of the Grenada invasion in 1984 by saluting those soldiers who gave their lives for freedom at the same time that he quietly let the one-year anniversary of the Beirut Marine Massacre pass unnoticed.

In April 1986 Reagan even instituted the first live prime-time bombing when he bombed Libya. His administration timed the bombing to begin at 7 P.M. New York time to cut into the national news. The national television media did not even realize how they had been manipulated.[79]

After the Reykjavic Summit in 1986, Donald Regan and others in the Reagan administration openly talked about how successful they had been in "damage control" and in getting "spin" for the administration's version as to what happened in Iceland between Soviet and American leaders. Of course, Reagan was more than capable of creating impressions that were favorable with carefully selected anecdotes which obscured reality. In 1983 a reporter asked President Reagan if he would comment on an "apparent continuing perception among a number of black leaders that the White House continues to be, if not hostile, at least not welcome to black viewpoints?" Reagan actually responded in the following fashion:

I'm aware of all that and it's very disturbing to me, because anyone who knows my life story knows that long before there was a thing called the civil rights movement, I was busy on that side. As a sports announcer, I didn't have any Willie Mays or Reggie Jacksons to talk about when I was broadcasting major-league baseball... And as a sports announcer I was one of a very small fraternity that used that job to editorialize against that ridiculous blocking of so many fine athletes and so many fine Americans from participating in what was called the great American game.[80]

The symbolic manipulation, of course, is that Reagan can personally show that he has no antiblack feelings without answering a substantive question related to policies of the Reagan administration.

The administration easily manipulated the American television and print media into an anti-Soviet frenzy after the downing of Korean Airlines flight 007. Moreover, the media became a pawn in Reagan's game to stir up anti-Libya propaganda from 1981 to 1985. Moreover, the Reagan administration proved to be master manipulators of image especially during campaigns. In 1984 the Reagan campaign commercials were generic all-American themes that stayed away from policy questions. They were subliminal messages to feel good about America and overt messages to feel good about Reagan.

Reagan became the quintessential media president. He was the complete triumph of image and style over substance. In 1982 Bruce Miroff published a most perceptive article, "Monopolizing the Public Space: The President as a Problem for Democratic Politics.[81] In Reagan's case, he not only monopolized public space, but he tried to manipulate it as well. In 1980 Reagan used a stolen debate briefing book to prepare for his debates with President Jimmy Carter. As Edward Pessen observed, this was similar to the time in college when Reagan was moved up to the second team in football after a scrimmage where a friend tipped him off in advance of all the offensive plays to be run by Reagan's opponents to make Reagan look better.[82] Before the debates, one of Reagan's debate coaches was ABC commentator George Will. This association was kept secret, and after the debate, Will dutifully announced that in his considered opinion, Reagan had "won" the debate against Carter.

The astonishing part about Reagan's efforts to manipulate the media was that he was so successful. In 1982 he told a predominately black high school in Chicago during a media event that he had made a mistake in trying to remove the IRS ability to cut off tax exemption for segregated schools. He told the students, "This is the first time that anyone's ever publicly asked me to try and explain what I was doing. . . . I was under the impression that the problem of segregated schools had been settled, and maybe I was wrong. I didn't know there were any court cases pending."[83] Then he continued with an incredible passage: "I've had to answer some of your questions with figures of what I claim are facts. Don't let me get away with it. Check me out. Make sure that what I told you checks out and is true. . . . Don't be the sucker generation."[84] With a president so skilled at remembering and reading script and with a national media that was so successfully manipulated at the early stages of his presidency, how could their generation have any other chance than being the "sucker generation?"

NOTES

1. Erving Goffman. *The Presentation of Self in Everyday Life* (New York: Anchor-Doubleday, 1959), p. 238.

2. Ibid.

3. Dan Nimmo. *Popular Images of Politics* (Englewood Cliffs, N.J.: Prentice-Hall, 1974), p. 132.

4. Ibid., p. 133.

5. Ibid., p. 134.

6. Ibid., p. 135.

7. Daniel Boorstin, *The Image: A Guide to Pseudo-Events In America* (New York: Harper and Row, 1964).

8. Ibid., pp. 39–40.

9. Ibid.

10. Ibid., p. 42.

11. Doris Graber, *Verbal Behavior and Politics* (Urbana: University of Illinois Press, 1976), pp. 229–233.

12. Boorstin, *The Image*, pp. 39–40.

13. Dan Nimmo, *Popular Images of Politics* (Englewood Cliffs, N.J.: Prentice-Hall, 1974), p. vii.

14. See Harold Lasswell, "The Native of Propaganda," in *Voice of the People*, ed. R. Christenson and W. McWilliams (New York: McGraw-Hill, 1962), pp. 320–324. See Harold Lasswell, D. Lerner, and I. Pool, *Comparative Study of Symbols* (Stanford, Calif.: Stanford University Press, Hoover Institute, 1952), and Harold Lasswell and J. Namenwirth, "The Changing Language of American Values: A Computer Study of Selected Party Platforms," in *Comparative Politics Series*, Vol. 1 (Beverly Hills, Calif.: Sage Professional Papers, 1970).

15. Lasswell, Lerner, and Pool, *Comparative Study of Symbols*, p. 12.

16. Harold Lasswell, *Politics: Who Gets What, When and How* (New York: World Publishing Company, 1958), p. 27.

17. Ibid., p. 13

18. Ibid., p. 31.

19. Harold Lasswell, N. Leites et al., *The Language of Politics* (Cambridge, Mass.: MIT Press, 1965), p. 8.

20. Murray Edelman, *The Symbolic Uses of Politics* (Urbana: University of Illinois Press, 1964), p. 6.

21. Murray Edelman, *Politics as Symbolic Action: Mass Arousal and Quiescence* (Chicago: Markham Publishing, 1971), p. 7.

22. Ibid., p. 17.

23. Ibid., p. 11.

24. Ibid., pp. 37–41.

25. Ibid., p. 41.

26. Donald Devine, *The Political Culture of the United States* (Boston: Little, Brown, 1972), pp. 105–134.

27. Richard Hamilton, *Class and Politics in the United States* (New York: John Wiley, 1972), p. 516.

28. Ibid., pp. 516–517.

29. Ibid., p. 517.

30. Dan Nimmo, *Popular Images of Politics* (Englewood Cliffs, N.J.: Prentice-Hall, 1974).

31. Richard Merelman "On the Neo-elitist Critique of Community Power," *American Political Science Review*, June 1968, pp. 451–461.

32. Ibid.

33. Roger Cobb and Charles Elder, *Participation in American Politics: The Dynamics of Agenda Building* (Boston: Allyn and Bacon, 1971).

34. Ibid., p. 93.

35. Ibid., p. 97.

36. Ibid., p. 151.

37. See Jack Dennis, ed., *Socialization to Politics* (New York: John Wiley, 1973). See Kent Jennings and Richard Niemi, *The Political Character of Adolescence* (Princeton, N.J.: Princeton University Press, 1974), and R. D. Hess and J. V. Torney, *The Development of Political Attitudes in Children* (Chicago: Aldine, 1967).

38. See Dennis, *Socialization for Politics*, 1973.

39. Fred Greenstein, "Popular Images of the Presidency," in A. Wildavsky, *The Presidency* (Boston: Little, Brown, 1969), pp. 286–295.

40. Alfred de Grazia, "The Myth of the President," in A. Wildavsky, *The Presidency*, pp. 49–73.

41. Thomas Cronin, "The Textbook Presidency and Political Science," paper delivered before American Political Science Association Annual Meeting, September 1970. See also Cronin, *The State of the Presidency*, 2d ed. (Boston: Little, Brown, 1980).

42. Bernard Kalb and Marvin Kalb, *Kissinger* (New York: Dell, 1973).

43. Richard Nixon, *The Real War* (New York: Warner Books, 1980), p. 250.

44. Robert Agranoff, *The Management of Election Campaigns* (Boston: Holbrook Press, 1976), pp. 3–6, and John W. Kingdon, *Candidates for Office: Beliefs and Strategies* (New York: Random House, 1968).

45. Thomas Patterson and Robert McClure, *The Unseeing Eye: The Myth of Television Power in National Politics* (New York: G. P. Putnam's Sons, 1976).

46. Robert Cantor, *Voting Behavior and Presidential Elections* (Itasca, Ill.: Peacock Publishers, 1975), pp. 104–105.

47. Philip Converse, "The Concept of the Normal Vote," in *Elections and the Political Order*, ed. Angus Campbell et al. (New York: John Wiley, 1966), pp. 9–39.

48. Lawrence Farley and John S. Marks, "Campaign Events and Electoral Outcomes," paper delivered at the American Political Science Association Annual Meeting, 1974.

49. Paul Lazarsfeld, Bernard Berelson, and Hazel Gaudet, *The People's Choice* (New York: Columbia University Press, 1944, 1948 and 1968). The 1968 Democratic convention and perhaps the 1976 Republican convention were counterproductive purposive media.

50. Agranoff, *Management of Election Campaigns*.

51. Ibid., p. 379.

52. The distinction is not always clear-cut. Sometimes "pure" political advertising is calculated to appear completely uncontrolled and spontaneous. Many elements of Nixon's 1968 campaign fit this description (see Joe McGinnes, *The Selling of the President* (New York: Trident, 1969).

53. Agranoff, *Management of Election Campaigns*, p. 341.

54. Manipulation of the media, and correspondingly public opinion, is not unique to the political candidate. Given the real and symbolic importance of the office, the presidency remains the most obvious showcase of media manipulation. See Elmer Cornwell, *Presidential Leadership of Public Opinion* (Bloomington: Indiana University Press, 1962); and David Wise, *The Politics of Living* (New York: Vintage, 1973).

55. Boorstin, *The Image*.

56. Doris Graber, *Verbal Behavior and Politics* (Urbana: University of Illinois Press, 1976), p. 249.

57. Boorstin, *The Image*, p. 11–12.

58. Jules Witcover, *Marathon* (New York: Viking, 1977), pp. 573–575.

59. Boorstin, *The Image*, p. 42.

60. L. Becker, M. McCombs, and J. McLeod, "The Development of Political Cognitions," in *Political Communication*, ed. Steven Chaffee (Beverly Hills, Calif.: Sage Publictions, 1975), pp. 21–64.

61. Lazarsfeld, Berelson, and Gaudet, *The People's Choice*.

62. See Leon Festinger, *A Theory of Cognitive Dissonance* (Stanford, Calif.: Stanford University Press, 1957); J. T. Klapper, *The Effects of Mass Communications* (New York: Free Press, 1960); and see Lewis Froman and John Skipper, "Factors Related to Misperceiving Party Stands on Issues," *Public Opinion Quarterly* 26 (1962): 265–271.

63. See Becker et al., "The Development of Political Cognitions," p. 28.

64. See S. Rosen, "Post-decision Affinity for Incompatible Information," *Journal of Abnormal and Social Psychology* 63 (1961): 188–190; David O. Sears, "Biased Indoctrination and Selectivity of Exposure to New Information," *Sociometry* 28 (1965): 363–376; and see J. L. Freedman, "Preference for Dissonant Information," *Journal of Personality and Social Psychology* 2 (1965): 287–289.

65. Sid Kraus, ed., *The Great Debates*, 2d ed. (Bloomingtom: Indiana University Press, 1977).

66. Paul Hagner and Leroy Rieselbach, "The Presidential Debates in the 1976 Campaign: A Panel Study," paper delivered at the Annual Meeting of the Midwest Political Science Association, Chicago, April 21–33, 1977.

67. Patterson and McClure, *The Unseeing Eye*.

68. Lazarsfeld, Berelson, and Gaudet, *The People's Choice*.

69. See Dan Nimmo, *The Political Persuaders* (Englewood Cliffs, N.J.: Prentice-Hall, 1970); David Sears and R. E. Witney, "Political Persuasion" in *Handbook of Communication*, ed. Poole and Schramm (Chicago: Rand McNally, 1973), pp. 253–286; and see Murray Edelman, "The Politics of Persuasion," in J. D. Barber's *Choosing the President* (Englewood Cliffs, N.J.: Prentice-Hall, 1974).

70. Edelman, "Politics of Persuasion," p. 154.

71. Sidney Verba and Norman Nie, *Participation in America* (New York: Harper and Row, 1972), pp. 174–208.

72. Edelman, "Politics of Persuasion," p. 152.

73. Haynes Johnson, "It was Wrong to Exclude the Press from the Grenada Invasion," *The Washington Post National Weekly Edition*, November 14, 1983, p. 29; Drew Middleton, "Barring Reporters from the Battlefield," *The New York Times Magazine*, February 5, 1984, pp. 36–37.

74. For a discussion of the secrecy-publicity continuum, see John Orman, *Presidential Secrecy and Deception: Beyond the Power to Persuade* (Westport, Conn.: Greenwood Press, 1980).

75. Stuart Taylor, Jr., "In Wake of Invasion, Much Official Misinformation by U.S. Comes to Light," *The New York Times*, November 6, 1983, p. 20.

76. William F. Mullen, *Presidential Power and Politics* (New York: St. Martin's Press, 1976), Chap. 4.

77. "Average Number of Press Conferences per Year," *Time*, March 30, 1987, p. 23.

78. James Deakin, "The Imperial President and the Imperial Media," in *Principles and Problems*, vol. 2, ed. Kenneth Thompson (New York: University Press of America, 1983); James Deakin, *Straight Stuff* (New York: William Morrow, 1984); and see John Tebbel and Sarah Miles

Watts, *The Press and the Presidency* (New York: Oxford University Press, 1985).

79. Tom Bower, "Was the Bombing of Tripoli a Misguided Vendetta by Reagan?" *The Listener*, April 2, 1987, p. 4.

80. James Nathan Miller, "Ronald Reagan and the Techniques of Deception," *The Atlantic Monthly*, February 1984, p. 68.

81. Bruce Miroff, "Monopolizing the Public space: The President as a Problem for Democratic Politics," in *Rethinking the Presidency*, ed. Thomas E. Cronin (Boston: Little, Brown, 1982).

82. Edward Pessen, *The Log Cabin Myth* (New Haven, Conn.: Yale University Press, 1984), pp. 134–135.

83. Miller, "Ronald Reagan and the Techniques of Deception," p. 64.

84. Ibid.

6

Reagan's Imperial Presidency

Historian Arthur Schlesinger, Jr., popularized the description "imperial" in his classic work, *The Imperial Presidency* to describe the systematic abuse of American presidential power.[1] Published in 1973, the book argued that the Johnson presidency of the 1960s and the Nixon presidency of the 1970s were the culmination of a long series of presidential power plays and aggrandizement. The examples of Vietnam and Watergate indicated that the American presidency had finally overindulged in its passion for grabbing power. Earlier, in the 1950s, Edward S. Corwin had argued that the whole history of the institution of the presidency had been one of "aggrandizement."[2] In expanding on Corwin's theme, Schlesinger argued that presidential power had been expanding ever since 1789. He argued that through various unusual exercises of presidential power, the advent of crisis diplomacy, the emergence of the United States as an industrial-military power in the twentieth century, and congressional abdication of its oversight responsibilities, the climate for the "imperial presidency" was created.

Schlesinger's thesis about the continuous trend toward excessively strong presidents in American history has been convincingly discredited by the "cyclical" theorists of American presidential power. Louis W. Koenig in his article "Reassessing the 'Imperial Presidency' " demonstrated that the history of presidential power has been one of fluctuation rather than one of continual aggrandize-ment. Richard Watson and Norman C. Thomas maintained that the presidency can best be described as "protean":

Like Proteus, the sea god in Greek mythology, the presidency is exceedingly *variable*, capable of assuming different shapes and forms. In line with the theatrical meaning of the term, presidents are "protean" players, assuming many roles in the political system as the circumstances demand.[3]

The ebb and flow of presidential power comes and goes as the political environment demands, according to James D. Barber in *The Pulse of Politics*.[4] Even Schlesinger in his book *The Cycles of History* has argued against a trend theory of presidential power.[5]

While one may argue with Schlesinger's theory of a historical trend toward "imperial presidencies," it is difficult to argue with the use of "imperial" to describe certain administrations. The im-perial president is one who is excessively secretive and deceptive, isolated and involved in the trappings of the office. The imperial president tries to manipulate the media, and he is decidedly anti–civil libertarian. The imperial president engages in unilateral war-making, and he is arrogant. Finally the imperial president engages in lawless behavior and generally is not held accountable for his actions.

Certainly the Ford and Carter presidencies could in no way be described as imperial, though they have been described as "post-imperial." Others have used the terms "imperiled" and "impossi-ble."[6] The Reagan presidency of the 1980s put an end to that kind of labeling. Reagan was said to have made the presidency work again. The return of strong presidential leadership was hailed by supporters and critics alike. Reagan showed that by narrowing one's agenda and by using all the bargaining chips that a president has in Neustadtian fashion, a president could make the institution work again.[7] Moreover, as this chapter argues, the Reagan presidency brought back something more than the return of strong, effective presidential leadership. It brought along a new kind of imperial presidency, one that was amiable and hidden so well that most observers missed it. Nevertheless, Reagan's presidency was one that was marked by excessive secrecy and deception, isolation and trap-pings, media manipulation and anti–civil libertarian posturing, unilateral warmaking and arrogance, lawlessness and the general lack of accountability. With apologies to Schlesinger's critics, there is no better word to describe this kind of behavior than "imperial."

Compared to the pack journalists reporting of Gerald Ford's and Jimmy Carter's "honeymoon," Reagan's first six months in office were consistently covered by the presidential watchers as the days of the "Super President."[8] The early successes of the Reagan administration were portrayed by the media as "victories" over Congress. These included victories with respect to tax cuts, domestic spending cuts, increased defense spending, and the sale of AWACs to Saudi Arabia. Most important, for the establishment of the Super President myth, Reagan survived an assassination attempt in his first year. It was noted that the Reagan presidency had indeed made the institution work again. Within six months, Reagan had restored visions of the "heroic" and "textbook" presidency.[9]

Even though 1982 brought about some increased media criticism during the biggest recession since the Great Depression in terms of unemployment, the media did not complain that the Reagan administration was an imperial presidency. Reagan was portrayed as the "Great Communicator" and as a friendly, likable, virile, patriotic leader. However, by the end of 1982 and certainly in 1983, some danger signs signaled the underside of Reagan's popular presidency. They were the signs of the "imperial presidency.'

The Reagan administration was not a friend to free speech, press, assembly, petition, and expression. In 1981 the administration moved to make it a crime to subscribe to the Cuban Communist party weekly, *Granma*, without a specific import license from the Treasury Department. The penalty for subscribing without a license could be $10,000 and ten years in prison because of the violation of the Trading with the Enemy Act of 1917.[10] The administration stopped the practice after losing a First Amendment lawsuit filed by the American Civil Liberties Union.

Under a Foreign Agents Registration Act of 1938, the Reagan administration required films produced under the direction of a foreign country that served a predominantly foreign interest to be labeled as "political propaganda." The Reagan Justice Department labeled one Canadian film "If You Love This Planet" (1983) as political propaganda. The offending message that served foreign interests was summarized in this way by the Justice Department:

"Unless we shake off our indifference and work to prevent nuclear war, we stand a slim chance of surviving the 20th century."[11]

The administration tried to make it difficult for scholars in the new high-tech areas to publish articles that cited unclassified documents. In 1982 the Defense Department prevented the publication of about 100 unclassified papers on "optical engineering" at an international symposium in California by warning that any presentation of "strategic" materials might be a violation of law.[12]

The cornerstone of the imperial presidency rests with the president's usurpation of the war powers by engaging in unilateral warmaking. The Reagan administration was essentially involved in unilateral warmaking in Grenada, Libya, and Nicaragua. He used overt acts of war to try to topple the leaders of these three countries. The last American president to try to destroy the leadership of three countries overtly by using acts of war was Franklin D. Roosevelt, who tried to topple the Axis powers during World War II. Of course, World War II was an officially declared war, and Roosevelt and Harry Truman were successful in their policy objectives, which had widespread American support. Reagan was able to overthrow only Grenada. In all three cases, Reagan did not have any authorization from Congress before he initiated military actions.

The Grenada invasion came two days after the October 2, 1983, terrorist bombing of a Marine barracks in Lebanon. It was a quintessential example of unilateral presidential warmaking. The administration did not consult Congress as mandated under the War Powers Act of 1973. Moreover, the Reagan administration did not "inform" appropriate members of Congress about the project until after the invasion had been launched. The action strengthened Reagan's role as commander-in-chief, and it indicated the limitations of Congress as a check against presidential warmaking.

The Reagan administration was one of the most arrogant in modern times. President Reagan simply did not admit mistakes. The diplomatic disaster of Bitburg in 1984 was never considered a mistake. Reagan's nuclear joke of 1984 to warm up the microphone announced that the Soviet Union had been outlawed and the bombing would begin in five minutes. The administration never apologized.

In 1982 the Reagan administration blamed the Carter administration for the hard economic recession. In 1983 after the bombing of the Marines in Beirut, the Reagan administration suggested that one of the reasons why the terrorists had surprised the U.S. troops was that the Carter administration had let U.S. intelligence capabilities lapse. He suggested that the Carter administration had also let U.S. defense and military readiness fall behind those of the Soviets. In 1984, candidate Reagan continued his "Carter bashing."

In 1983, Reagan fired three members of the six-person Civil Rights Commission for monitoring the administration's nonenforcement of civil rights laws. No other president had ever done this. At a press conference in that same year, Reagan talked about the right of Americans to speak out about their "concerns." He said, "Let us always remember, with that privilege goes a responsibility to be right."[13] He warned anti-nuclear demonstrators that he would not be moved by their mass demonstration in New York, Washington, and elsewhere in 1982. It was the arrogance of the imperial president.

As Pat Schroeder, U.S. Representative from Colorado, observed in 1983, Reagan was the "Teflon president" because nothing ever seemed to stick. Whenever charges of corruption and conflicts of interest came about during the Reagan administration, the charges never attacked the president. Indeed, it was always Ray Donovan, Michael Deaver, or William Casey who had to defend themselves on the "sleaze factor" of the Reagan administration. It was never hinted that Reagan might have to answer for the ethics of his friends.

With this pre-Irangate track record, the Reagan administration in October 1986 was preparing the "spin" for presidential greatness. Reagan's second term was moving along with an eye toward his standing in history. Much like Richard Nixon, Reagan tried to manipulate events with a concern for "image" of presidential greatness. By November 1986 the Reagan magic in hiding the imperial presidency began to fall apart as the administration had to defend itself against allegations in the affair that soon acquired the nickname "Irangate." Irangate highlighted the characteristics of the imperial presidency better than any previous isolated incidents of imperial behavior.

The Reagan presidency has provided interesting presidential watching for all observers of the American presidency. British writers and scholars have been among these students since long before Reagan and have produced some of the most perceptive examinations. In 1888 (1st ed.) James Bryce in his *The American Commonwealth* explained why great men in the United States were not chosen president.[14] Harold Laski offered his interpretations of the institution in his book, *The American Presidency* in 1940.[15] Laski clearly had found an activist in Franklin Roosevelt, and the Roosevelt presidency clearly influenced his views greatly. More recently, journalist Godfrey Hodgson presented one of the best cases for the "no-win" presidency in his important book *All Things to All Men: The False Promise of the American President* in 1980.[16] In fact Reagan's presidency gives ample evidence to the views of Bryce, Laski, and Hodgson. Bryce might have seen Reagan as another example of the system's inability to elect a great man. Laski might have been impressed by Reagan's ability to have an impact on his times in the manner that Roosevelt influenced his times, although Laski would have surely disagreed with the direction Reagan took the country. Hodgson's thesis of the no-win, impossible presidency seems to apply to the Reagan presidency especially in the light of the Iran-Contra scandal.

The Reagan presidency was cause for alarm for some Europeans and for some British people in particular. Reagan did not inspire confidence, and he did not even do as well as former President Jimmy Carter in convincing the British public that he was an effective leader. The Reagan years showed a slight decrease in confidence in the United States as measured by the Gallup survey of Britain in 1986.

Reagan was a target for the famed British social satirists, most notably by the "Splitting Image" puppets. Reagan was often portrayed as just an actor, a "trigger-happy war monger," "senile," "naive," a "macho simpleton," or worse. While Labour party supporters almost uniformly had negative views of Ronald Reagan, and while most Alliance party backers disliked Reagan's presidency, the Tory voters and the Margaret Thatcher supporters tended to view Reagan in positive terms as a strong leader.

As one U.S. journalist observed about the British, they really did not know what to make of the Reagan presidency. Don Bonafede of the *National Journal* summarized his observations after attending a British conference on the Reagan presidency:

Perhaps the most vivid impression is that after more than five years, Europeans still don't know what to make of Ronald Reagan. That the President doesn't easily fit any preconceived mold and has, at times, acted contrary to expectations seem to sorely vex them.

During a conference on "The Reagan Years" at Oxford University, sponsored by the American Politics Group here and attended by many of Britain's most prominent political scientists, it was evident they have never forgiven the President for having been a Hollywood actor. "How," a participant inquired, "can the American people take seriously a former film actor?"[17]

Bonafede felt that the British did not understand the importance of Reagan's personality and style in running the presidency. He noted,

British academics, however, appear to be on shaky ground in assessing the presidency as an institution. They ignore the fact that a President's power lies less in the constitutional and statutory provisions than in his personal vision and character and his ability to communicate and influence the mass of the electorate and thus create a national coalition. They tend to reject the notion that a President's style and personality and how he acts can be as significant as what he does. The fact that the presidency is an office both institutionalised and personalised seems to elude them.[18]

Given this negative environment for the perception of Reagan's presidential performance to 1986, it is little wonder then that the Irangate scandal served as ample evidence to confirm some British people's worst fears about Ronald Reagan. The British press covered Irangate as a major international story. As expected, *The Guardian*, the most liberal daily newspaper in England, attributed the worst motives to Reagan's actions, but as the story unraveled in the United States, this kind of analysis became the standard approach to reporting the scandal in *The Times*, *The Observer*, and other papers.

The English correspondents followed the pack instincts of the American press that normally covers the American president and kept the British reading public aware of the Iran-Contra scandal. News on television channels like BBC 1 and ITN dramatized the events for British viewers. In February journalists Michael White and Alex Brummer for *The Guardian* and Michael Binyon for *The Times* prepared readers for the results of the Tower Commission report. Fred Halliday traced "Reagan's Doctrine of Deceit" and Christopher Thomas of *The Times* wrote about the isolated Reagan presidency. In general Reagan was portrayed as a president who was out of touch with his staff and with reality. The Tower Commission revelations were duly noted in the British press, but new attention was given to the Reagan attack on Qaddafi. Reagan was accused of trying to assassinate the Libyan leader during the air strike on Libya.[19]

One perceptive journalist, Simon Jenkins of the *Sunday Times*, observed that the lesson of Irangate for Britain was not for British people to be smug about the political mistakes of the leader of the "free world," but rather that Britain should learn the positive lessons of a political system that had the ability to investigate alleged wrongdoing without the Official Secrets Act that dominates much of British politics.[20]

Reagan was called befuddled, bemused, bewildered, a puppet, inattentive, and a zombie by the British writers on the American presidency after the Tower Commission report was released. The personal tragedy of Robert McFarlane and his suicide attempt also received press attention. Nancy Reagan was portrayed as the "dragon lady" who ran the White House Chief of Staff Donald Regan out of office and as a woman who wanted her husband to pursue arms control in order to get the press off her husband's shortcomings during Irangate.[21]

Simon Hoggart wrote about "Shattering of King Ronnie's Fantasy World" as the British press detailed the upcoming institutional investigations into alleged wrongdoing by the Reagan administration.[22] Much emphasis was put on a possible coverup that would let Reagan escape accountability by appearing to be unaware of actions taken by Oliver North. He was called a "lame-duck," marginal caretaker, a liar, a charade player, image manipulator, and pathetic.[23]

His staff, especially Oliver North, were labeled as cowboys, sleazy men, ideologues, criminals, and conspirators in the British press.[24] By the summer of 1987 the British press and the television media kept British citizens fully informed about the Irangate hearings. BBC television and especially ITN would wrap up the activities of the day's hearings in Washington by playing the best videotape exchanges between witnesses and members of the congressional committee. The story of Oliver North and his media success in the United States was told over and over. However, Oliver North did not become an overnight matinee hero in England as he did in the United States. His rise as an American hero was down right scary to many British citizens. It was not explainable, and it was hard to believe, according to most British reports on Oliver North's fame. One paper wrote an editorial called "North Wind" and asked how could anyone seriously or even jokingly suggest that Oliver North was presidential timber for the 1988 presidential election in the United States. The British press viewed the man as a criminal, and they could not understand how the American press could detail North's victory of image and style over substance and content.[25]

North was covered as "the fall guy to good guy," and reporters tried to explain "the meaning of Ollie-mania."[26] Christopher Hitchens called the story "the adoration of the mad guy," and Ambrose Evans-Pritchard labeled it "Oliver's Twist."[27] Michael White called it "Olliewood."[28] It was a reminder to British readers just how gullible the American people could be.

Another story that related to the show-biz mentality of American politics and the process the American political system engages in was the Gary Hart story. The British press savored this story more than usual. After all, the line on scandals was that the British had sexual scandals in their political system, and Americans only embarrassed themselves over greed or ideology. Now the Americans had a full-blown sex scandal of their own. Not only Fleet Street tabloids had a good time at Hart's expense, but the major media in England also had fun with the story. *The Guardian* took time to point out the failure of the American nomination system, and *The Times* covered it as "Bowled Over by a Bimbo."[29] Hart and Donna Rice were front-page news in England for almost a week in May 1987.

The British press covers American politics in a serious, sustained manner, much more than the American press covers the British political system. the American system and its current events are often regarded in disbelief. How could the so-called leader of the free world have a system of politics that operates like the American political system? British journalists often wonder. Nevertheless, the British press corps continues the coverage and often reports stories that are not given much emphasis back in the United States. For example, British journalists wrote about the distinct probability that CIA agent James Buckley was tortured and murdered in Teheran,

Iran, rather than in captivity in Lebanon. More explosively, the British press wrote that the first shipments of American-made military parts went to Iran in February 1981, not in 1985 as stated in the Tower Commission report. Some writers speculated that William Casey had made a deal with Iran to release the American hostages when Reagan became president in January 1981, and then they would get American equipment as a quid pro quo.

Finally British journalist Jon Snow summarized his feelings about what it was like for a British journalist to be watching Irangate unfold in the United States. Snow told *Mother Jones* in the summer of 1987 that he felt that U.S. journalists had been taken in by the so-called Reagan magic. The U.S. media focused on Reagan's style, image, personality, and popularity without doing the digging that was necessary to report what Reagan was really doing. Snow observed,

as an outsider, it's easy to find fault with the way the American media have approached the Reagan presidency. In doing so I am only too well aware that I write from the midst of a culture that most assuredly would have tried much harder to prevent its own equivalent scandal from seeing the light of day. It is precisely because the American media have established such a lead in press freedom, and in reporting dishonesty in government, that those of us who depend upon that lead lose heart when we see past achievement undermined by present failure.[30]

Irangate and the Gary Hart story were further evidence to many British citizens as reported by the British press and television, that the American presidency had serious problems. These problems were viewed as a continuation of others for American presidential politics including the Vietnam syndrome, Watergate, and the CIA/FBI revelations of 1976. Irangate just continued the story of failed presidencies.

NOTES

1. Arthur M. Schlesinger, Jr., *The Imperial Presidency* (Boston: Houghton Mifflin, 1973).

2. Edward S. Corwin, *The President: Office and Powers* (New York: NYU Press, 1957), pp. 29–30.

3. Richard A. Watson and Norman C. Thomas, *The Politics of the Presidency* (New York: John Wiley, 1984), p. 16.

4. James D. Barber, *The Pulse of Politics* (New York: Norton, 1980).

5. Arthur Schlesinger, Jr., *Cycles of History* (Boston: Houghton Mifflin, 1986).

6. Thomas Cronin, "An Imperiled Presidency?" in *The Post-Imperial Presidency*, ed. Vincent Davis (New Brunswick, N.J.: Transaction Books, 1980). See also Godfrey Hodgson, *All Things to All Men: The False Promise of the Modern Presidency* (New York: Simon and Schuster, 1980), and Harold M. Barger, *The Impossible Presidency* (Glenview, Ill.: Scott, Foresman, 1984).

7. Richard E. Neustadt, *Presidential Power* (New York: John Wiley, 1960 and 1980 editions).

8. John Orman, *Comparing Presidential Behavior* (Westport, Conn.: Greenwood Press, 1987).

9. Watson and Thomas, *The Politics of the Presidency*, pp. 3–6.

10. Walter Karp, "Liberty Under Siege," *Harper's*, November 1985, p. 55.

11. Floyd Abrams, "The New Effort to Control Information," *The New York Times Magazine*, September 25, 1983, p. 24.

12. Ibid., p. 27.

13. Karp, "Liberty Under Siege," p. 63.

14. James Bryce, *The American Commonwealth*, 2d ed. (New York: Macmillan, 1893).

15. Harold Laski, *The American Presidency: An Interpretation* (London: George Allen and Unwin, 1940).

16. Godfrey Hodgson, *All Things to All Men* (London: Weidenfeld and Nicolson, 1980).

17. Don Bonafede, "Conference Report," *American Politics Group Newsletter*, no. 16 (June 1986): 10.

18. Ibid., p. 11.

19. See Michael White, "White House Prepares for Harsh Report on Irangate," *The Guardian*, February 14, 1987, p. 7; Alex Brummer, "New Irangate Charges," *The Guardian*, February 20, 1987, p. 1; Michael Binyon, "Iran Scandal Engulfs Reagan and Casey," *The Times*, February 17, 1987, p. 7; Fred Halliday, "Reagan's Doctrine of Deceit," *The Guardian*, February 13, 1987, p. 11; Christopher Thomas, "Reclusive Reagan Isolates Himself from Press," *The Times*, February 16, 1987, p. 1; Jon Connell and Will Ellsworth-Jones, "Reagan Tried to Kill Gadaffi," *Sunday Times*, February 22, 1987, p. 1.

20. Simon Jenkins, "Irangate's Lesson for Britain," *Sunday Times*, February 22, 1987, p. 25.

21. See "Befuddled, Bemused and Bewildered," *The Guardian*, February 27, 1987, p. 10; Simon Hoggart, "The Zombie President," *The Observer*, March 1, 1987, p. 11; Christopher Thomas, "Triumphant Mrs. Reagan Pursues Arms Control," *The Times*, March 4, 1987, p. 9.

22. Simon Hoggart, "Shattering of King Ronnie's Fantasy World," *The Observer*, March 8, 1987, p. 13.

23. Alex Brummer, "World Passes by the Caretaker of the Marginal White House," *The Guardian*, May 15, 1987, p. 8; Simon Hoggart, "Charade in the Oval Office," *The Observer*, March 29, 1987, p. 11.

24. John Connell, "Dead Men Tell No Tales—but the Cowboy Show Rolls On," *The Times*, May 10, 1987, p. 14; Patrick Brogan, "Spotlight on All the President's Sleazy Men," *The Observer*, May 3, 1987, p. 15.

25. "North Wind," editorial, *Eastern Daily Press*, July 11, 1987, p. 12.

26. Anthony Sampson, "The Meaning of Ollie-Mania," *Newsweek* (international), July 27, 1987, p. 10.

27. Christopher Hitchens, "The Adoration of the Mad Guy," *New Statesman*, July 17, 1987, p. 20, and see Ambrose Evans-Pritchard, "Oliver's Twist Saves Reagan," *The Spectator*, July 18, 1987, pp. 9–11.

28. Michael White, "Olliewood Scores as TV Soap," *The Guardian*, July 9, 1987, p. 1.

29. Paul Bailey, "Bowled Over by a Bimbo," *The Times*, May 10, 1987, p. 51.

30. Jon Snow, "A Visitor in King Ronnie's Court," *Mother Jones*, June/July 1987, p. 42.

7

The Loss of Presidential Accountability

This book has surveyed the state of affairs in keeping the president accountable through the Reagan years. Five major areas of concern still persist. As chapter 2 demonstrated, American presidents have a very poor record in defending individual liberties of American citizens. Given the permanent national security state that the United States has become since World War II, one should not expect American presidents to change their behavior to become defenders of their opposition's right to mobilize. Chapter 3 detailed the specific problems for democratic accountability of the chief executive that are posed by the intelligence community. To the degree a country is willing to legitimize covert operations beyond just gathering intelligence, it automatically sacrifices presidential accountability. Another potential problem for presidential accountability, as seen in chapter 4, is the problem of the abuse of the president's discretionary power in the criminal justice arena. This allows the president to politicize justice in America. In chapter 5, the serious problem of celebrity politics and trivialization encourages the president to act as the nation's top celebrity. The president uses symbolic manipulation within the celebrity political system to promote his image and to divert those who want him to account for his actions. Finally, chapter 6 discussed the problems for presidential accountability that are posed by a popular, amiable president like Ronald Reagan.

Given these new and recurring problems for presidential accountability, it is clear that in the 1990s the American political system has lost the desire and the power to keep presidents accountable. Even though Congress attempted to reassert its power in relation to the runaway presidency in the 1970s by passing measures like the Case Act (1972), the War Powers Act (1973), the Hughes-Ryan Amendment (1974), the Campaign Finance Act (1974), the Budget and Impoundment Control Act (1974), and the National Emergencies Act (1976), these acts did not change the conditions that give strong encouragement to the president to engage in secret and deceptive behavior.

Bert Rockman has observed that the issue of presidential accountability comes up only after some abuse of presidential power that occurs in cyclical fashion in American politics. He wrote:

It is not sufficient to ask whether the president has too much or too little power as such, for that frequently ebbs and flows with our judgments of particular incumbents and our likes and dislikes of what they are trying to achieve. Moreover, the fact is that presidents in our times tend to get about as far as their supply of popular support allows. Popular politics is the fuel driving presidential governance.[1]

Yet the institution of the postmodern presidency has changed because of the new political environment.[2] American presidents in the 1990s must partake in a presidency where actual powers of the institution do not meet the expectations and responsibilities that many citizens have for the office. In an era of the decline of the U.S. empire, American presidents can no longer influence events in an uncertain world. Presidents cannot control the economy. Presidents cannot control domestic policy except through force of personality and timing. Presidents cannot control the Supreme Court, the international economy, American allies, or events in the Third World. The only field of control left for presidents is secretive and deceptive covert operations in foreign and domestic policy. Moreover, presidents in the postmodern presidency have extraordinary advantages in attempting to manipulate public opinion.

The postmodern presidency has become the "plebiscitary presidency" according to Theodore Lowi.[3] The three major assumptions of this model for the presidency are that (1) the state and the president are one and the same; the president is the state personified, (2) presidential powers should be commensurate with expectations put upon the president, and (3) the president cannot and should not be bound by the same law that binds ordinary citizens.[4]

The president who moved the postmodern presidency most toward the plebiscitary model was Richard Nixon. Despite his enormous failure in containing the Watergate coverup and his numerous illegalities, which cost him the presidency, Nixon's operating style on how to run the plebiscitary presidency influenced Ford, Carter, especially Reagan, and then Bush. In theory, what could be more democratically accountable than a plebiscitary model for the presidency? Bert Rockman asks.[5] The president is held accountable by the American people as popular sovereignty becomes the crucial source of democratic accountability. Public opinion serves to constrain presidential behavior, in theory.

The theory of accountability by the people, however, is flawed. Presidents can lie, withhold information, and systematically try to manipulate public opinion. This was Richard Nixon's operational mode for the presidency. His impact on the postmodern presidency cannot be underestimated. His legacy continued through the Reagan and Bush administrations.

Perhaps no book illustrates Nixon's approach to the plebiscitary presidency better than his own secret files. Edited by Bruce Oudes, the book *From: The President . . . Richard Nixon's Secret Files* provides the best raw material for an inside look at the operating style of the postmodern presidency.[6] Nixon reveals an obsession for polls, television manipulation, direct miscommunication with the electorate, presidential symbols, pseudo-events, speech writers, image consultants, and public relations in the plebiscitary presidency.

As early as January 9, 1969, Nixon wrote a memo to Haldeman and Ehrlichman asking that the administration develop an objective capability to analyze the content and pictorial slant of the 1968 campaign as it impacted voters. He wanted an in-depth operation to provide the very latest in polling information.[7] He wanted a full-time presidential media tape library, so that he could view coverage of the president on television. He wanted to control the pictures that would emerge as the TV record of his administration. He would decide about photo opportunities, timing, locations, and backdrops. How would the prisoners-of-war play? What would the Great Wall of China look like in prime time? Nixon's attention to symbolic manipulation in the presidency established the precedents for television manipulation of the electorate by controlled media. Later, Ronald Reagan would move beyond Nixon and establish new precedents for symbolic manipulation. The "public relations" presidency is what the post modern presidency revolves around.

As Thomas Cronin has observed, "Presidential television has produced a troubling problem for democratic politics."[8] The problem, best stated by Bruce Miroff is "public awareness of issues is largely governed by the problems he [the president] has defined and the battles he is engaged in fighting. His role in the public space is so prominent that it is sometimes hard for others simply to be seen on any large scale."[9]

Even in classic live encounters in the media, over which presidents supposedly do not have absolute control, the video president has an opportunity to score points. As Bob Schieffer and Gary Gates have reported, George Bush's great confrontation with Dan Rather over the Iran-Contra affair during live television was the quintessential example of the candidate standing up to the huge media superanchors and scoring with the public. However, this event was not the spontaneous exchange it was portrayed to be by media accounts in earlier versions. According to Schieffer and Gates, Bush's media advisor Roger Ailes had stationed himself next to the camera and was writing out key responses on a legal pad so that Bush would give the correct response.[10]

The popular plebiscitary president can escape the law in certain situations. Even through Richard Nixon was impeached on three counts by the House Judiciary Committee in 1974, his influence on the Reagan presidency was monumental. Reagan's behavior during his presidency was so Nixonian in many ways that a few of the specifics in the Articles of Impeachment against Nixon even apply to him. He, of course, was never called upon to account for his actions in a court of law or under oath, but by rewording various sections of Nixon's Articles of Impeachment, one can see that they could easily apply to Ronald Reagan.[11]

When Ronald Reagan left the White House in January 1989 to retire to California, he left an American presidency that refused to account to anyone. His former national security advisor John Poindexter claimed he had created "plausible deniability" in his testimony to the Iran-Contra Joint Committee by refusing to inform President Reagan about Oliver North and William Casey's effort to resupply the Contras during the restrictive period of the Boland Amendment (1984–1986). However, few citizens believed that Ronald Reagan had told the true story of Iran-Contra. Moreover, it appeared that there was no mechanism, except for Reagan's memoirs, where the former president would have to testify under oath about what he knew about the efforts to circumvent the Boland Amendment.

In May 1989 Reagan's trusted cowboy Oliver North was convicted by a jury in the District of Columbia on two charges of obstructing Congress by shredding documents and one charge of accepting an illegal gratuity. He was acquitted on nine other charges relating to the Iran-Contra affair, as the jurors apparently believed that North was acting on orders from his superiors. During the trial documents became available for the first time that indicated that Ronald Reagan and his vice-president George Bush had wider knowledge of the effort to resupply the Contras than was previously believed.

The Tower Commission and the final report of the Iran-Contra Joint Committee did not portray Ronald Reagan or George Bush as being major players in the covert resupply effort. That was supposed to be the end of all the systemic questions about presidential and vice-presidential responsibility in the 1980s era of accountability. Yet nagging questions about Reagan's role and Bush's role continued to be unanswered.

In the era of celebrity politics of the 1980s, the fragile mechanisms to hold the president and the vice-president accountable for their actions dramatically failed. The media were unable to get Reagan or Bush to talk about their involvement. The Tower Commission could not serve as an instrument of presidential accountability because Reagan and Bush were not treated as central players in the affair. The Iran-Contra Joint Committee was unable to handle Oliver North's testimony that turned the tide of the investigation. Finally, the committee was reduced to the absurd position of accepting Poindexter's testimony that he had not informed the president because the committee refused to subpoena President Reagan or Vice-President Bush to get them to testify under oath. Judge Gerhard Gesell refused to allow Reagan and Bush to be subpoenaed for the Oliver North trial. Opposition candidates like Robert Dole and Alexander Haig in the 1988 Republican primaries could not get George Bush to account for his role in the Iran-Contra affair. Michael Dukakis was unable to focus national attention on Bush's role in the scandal during the 1988 presidential election. Even the usually reliable presidential watchdog, media anchor Dan Rather, was unable to get Bush to account for his actions during his famous live interview confrontation with candidate Bush.

The system did not work the way it did during Watergate or the CIA/FBI revelations of the 1970s, when in many respects, the secret government coup pulled off by the Reagan administration was every bit as much of a threat to constitutional government in the United States as the two scandals of the 1970s were. The problems of keeping presidents accountable, as this book has demonstrated, contain enduring elements like presidential secrecy and deception to be sure, but the problem for the 1990s is compounded by the rise of the president's ability to manipulate political symbols and to engage in celebrity politics. This powerful combination of anti-democratic tendencies could threaten American freedom, civil liberties, and justice in the 1990s.

Unless citizens and institutions keep asking the important questions about presidential behavior, future presidents will come to believe that these types of anti-democratic actions are acceptable in American democracy. If no one complains, or if the media and the public think the president or vice-president is a "nice, popular guy," the presidents can persist in unaccountable behavior.

George Bush has learned his lessons well. If Ronald Reagan was the "Teflon president," then George Bush can be seen as the latest high-tech Teflon. He has shown an ability to dodge the effects of potentially damaging political scandals. It was not the best time to serve, but he served as Republican party national chairman during some of the Nixon years, and served as CIA director for President Ford during the Year of Intelligence (1975–76) to keep the agency together when the revelations of past behavior became public. Finally, he was elected to the presidency without the Iran-Contra scandal costing him any significant support.

Perhaps the questions surrounding the Iran-Contra scandal will never be answered. Perhaps it is the ultimate successful coverup of presidential wrongdoing. The serious indictment of the political system is not so much that the coverup was successful, but that most citizens, commentators, responsible elected officials, presidential watchers, and media analysts did not care if the coverup was successful. Reagan and Bush were popular presidents, and many actors in the political system did not have the political courage to go for the jugular. Some felt that too many presidents had already been bashed. Some felt that the country had to stop "wallowing in Iran-Contra" and get on with other business. Some felt it was possible that Reagan and Bush might not have known about the efforts to resupply the Contras. Finally, others just did not care.

Given this loss of accountability for popular presidents in the 1980s, it behooves citizens who still believe the idea that no person is above the law to become more vigilant in the 1990s to keep a check on runaway presidential behavior. That would probably be one of the best ways citizens could celebrate the 200th anniversary of the Bill of Rights in 1991.

NOTES

1. Bert Rockman, "Studying the American Presidency in the Bicentennial Year," *Presidency Research 5*, no. 1 (Fall 1987): 13.

2. See Richard Rose, "The Post-Modern Presidency: The World Closes in on the White House," *Presidency Research 10*, no. 2 (Spring 1988): 5–8; and see Ryan Barilleaux, "Post-Modern American Presidency," 10, no. 1 (Fall 1987): 15–18.

3. Theodore Lowi, "Presidential Power: Restoring the Balance," *Political Science Quarterly* 100, no. 2 (Summer 1985): 189.

4. Ibid.

5. Bert Rockman, "The Modern Presidency and Theories of Accountability: Old Wine and Old Bottles," paper presented at the Annual Meeting of the American Political Science Association, Washington, D.C., August 28–31, 1986, p. 37.

6. Bruce Oudes, ed. *From: The President . . . Richard Nixon's Secret Files* (New York: Harper and Row, 1989).

7. Ibid., pp. 2–3.

8. Thomas Cronin, ed., *Rethinking the Presidency* (Boston: Little, Brown, 1982).

9. Bruce Miroff, "Monopolizing the Public Space: The President as a Problem for Democratic Politics," in Cronin, ed., *Rethinking the Presidency*, pp. 99–100.

10. Bob Schieffer and Gary Gates, "That Bush-Rather Blowup: A New Twist," *TV Guide*, July 8–14, 1989, p. 35.

11. Among the specific charges against Richard Nixon in the House Judiciary Articles of impeachment which apply to Reagan—and George Bush for that matter—are

1. making or causing to be made false or misleading statements

2. withholding relevant and material evidence from lawfully authorized investigative officers and employees of the United States

3. endeavoring to misuse the Central Intelligence Agency, an Agency of the United States

4. making false or misleading public statements for the purpose of deceiving the people of the United States into believing that a thorough and complete investigation had been conducted with respect to allegations of misconduct on the part of personnel of the executive branch of the United States

5. contempt of Congress.

Nixon was impeached on these counts and others. Of course, President Reagan and then President Bush were never formally charged with any of these impeachable offenses. Moreover, Reagan and Bush were never formally asked to account for the shipment of arms to Iran in February 1981, less than one month after the hostages were returned to Teheran.

Selected Bibliography

REAGAN'S IMPERIAL PRESIDENCY

Associated Press, "President Said Briefed by North." *The Bridgeport Post,* December 6, 1986, pp. 6–7.

Broder, David. "Ending Presidential Paranoia." *The Bridgeport Telegram,* November 20, 1986, p. 18.

Conason, Joe, and Murray Waas. "What Casey Knew: The CIA and the Secret Contra Network." *The Village Voice,* December 16, 1986, pp. 17–22, plus.

"Editors Protest to White House." *New York Times,* October 13, 1986, p. A11.

Engelberg, Stephen. "Congress Plans to Investigate Covert Policies." *New York Times,* November 9, 1986, pp. 1 and 10.

———. "White House says CIA had a Role in Iran Operation," *New York Times,* November 15, 1986, p. 1.

Genovese, Michael. "The Return of the Imperial Presidency." *Presidency Research* 8 (Winter 1986).

Hamill, Pete. "Body Bag of Lies." *The Village Voice.* December 30, 1986, p. 10.

"High Crimes and Misdemeanors." *Mother Jones,* February/March 1987, pp. 6–7.

Horrock, Nicholas. "Bloodied But Unbeaten, Reagan Must Now Restore Credibility." *The Bridgeport Post,* November 23, 1986, p. A2.

Horrock, Nicholas, and George DeLuma. "Reagan's Use of Covert Tactics Draws Fire: Inefficiencies Cited." *The Bridgeport Post*, November 16, 1986, p. A2.

Karp, Walter. "Liberty Under Siege." *Harper's*, November 1985, pp. 53–67.

LeMoyne, James. "Central America Asks How Far U.S. Will Go." *The New York Times*, November 2, 1986, p. E3.

Lewis, Anthony. "The Reasons for Lying." *The New York Times*, October 13, 1986, p. A19.

———. "The Rule of Law (II)." *The New York Times*, January 9, 1984, p. A17.

Mauro, Tony. "Legality of Iran Deal Questioned." *USA Today*, November 21, 1986, p. 6A.

Morrow, Lance. "Yankee Doodle Magic: What Makes Reagan so Remarkably Popular a President?" *Time*, July 7, 1986, pp. 12–16.

Neuman, Johanna. "Correction Follows Press Talk," *USA Today*, November 20, 1986, p. 5A.

Neuman, Johanna, and Patrick O'Driscoll. "President's Credibility on Firing Line." *USA Today*, November 19, 1986, p. 1.

Pear, Robert. "Assembling Some of the Pieces of the Puzzle." *The New York Times*, December 14, 1986, Section 4, pp. 1–2.

———. "Court Is Asked to Define Power of the Pocket Veto." *The New York Times*, November 9, 1986, p. 4E.

"Reagan on TV." *USA Today*, November 20, 1986, p. 11A.

Reeves, Richard. "Blacklist Cover-up." *The Bridgeport Post*, March 2, 1984, p. 10.

Reston, James. "How to Fool the People." *The New York Times*, October 5, 1986, p. 21E.

Ridgeway, James. "Home Is Where the Covert Action Is: Harassment of Peace Groups Raises Questions." *The Village Voice*, December 16, 1986, p. 24.

Schneider, Keith. "North's Record: A Wide Role in a Host of Sensitive Projects." *The New York Times*, January 3, 1987, p. 1.

Shipler, David. "The Iran Connection." *The New York Times*, November 16, 1986, Section 4, p.1.

Weinraub, Bernard. "Criticism on Iran and Other Issues Puts Reagan's Aides on Defensive." *The New York Times*, November 16, 1986, p. 1.

"White House Reduces Media Access to Reagan." *The Bridgeport Post*, July 10, 1986, p. 12.

Wieseltier, Leon. "What Went Wrong? An Appraisal of Reagan's Foreign Policy." *The New York Times Magazine*, December 7, 1986, pp. 43–47.

REAGAN'S SECRECY

Abrams, Floyd. "The New Effort to Control Information." *The New York Times Magazine*, September 25, 1983, pp. 22–28.

Associated Press, "Caution Urged on Reagan's Lie Detector Order." *The Bridgeport Post*, December 12, 1985, p. 7.

"CIA Seeks to Control Material." *The Bridgeport Post*, May 7, 1986, p. 4.

Earley, Pete. "The Man Who Keeps the Secrets." *Washington Post National Weekly Edition*, January 2, 1984, p. 29.

Hundley, Kris. "Official U.S. Disinformation." *Fairfield County Advocate*, November 3, 1986, p. 9.

Johnson, Haynes. "It Was Wrong to Exclude the Press from the Grenada Invasion." *Washington Post National Weekly Edition*, November 14, 1983, p. 29.

Lardner, George, Jr. "Federal Officials Are Facing 'Random' Lie Detector Tests." *The Washington Post National Weekly Edition*, November 7, 1983, p. 37.

Lelyveld, Joseph. "The Director: Running the CIA." *The New York Times Magazine*, January 20, 1985, pp. 16–28.

Maraniss, David. "New Fronts in the Old War Against Leaks and Disclosure." *The Washington Post National Weekly Edition*, November 28, 1983, pp. 6–7.

Middleton, Drew. "Barring Reporters from the Battlefield." *The New York Times Magazine*, February 5, 1984, pp. 36–37.

Miller, James Nathan. "Ronald Reagan and the Techniques of Deception." *The Atlantic Monthly*, February 1984, pp. 62–68.

Miller, Judith. "Putting It All Together, Critics Spell." *The New York Times*, November 15, 1981, p. 2E.

"More Secrets." *The Washington Post National Weekly Edition*, May 27, 1985, p. 29.

"Reagan Delays Orders for Lie Detector Use." *The Bridgeport Post*, February 15, 1984, p. 6.

Reeves, Richard. "Police State, U.S.A." *The Bridgeport Post*, January 2, 1986, p. 14.

Roberts, Steven. "Senator Says the Administration Is Withholding Intelligence Data." *The New York Times*, March 17, 1982, p. A14.

Schorr, Daniel. "The Administration's Unofficial Secrets Act." *The New York Times*, August 3, 1986, p. E23.

Taylor, Stuart, Jr. "Administration Seeks a Stronger Lock on 'Classified' Files." *The New York Times*, March 24, 1985, p.. E5.

———. "In Wake of Invasion, Much Official Misinformation by U.S. Comes to Light." *The New York Times*, November 6, 1983, p. 20.

"U.S. Still Blacklists 3,000 Canadians for Politics." *The New York Times,* February 19, 1984.

Woodward, Bob. "Reagan Tells Casey He May Stay on as CIA Chief in a New Term." *The Washington Post National Weekly Edition,* September 24, 1984, p. 31.

REAGAN'S WAR AGAINST NICARAGUA

Alpern, David, et al. "America's Secret Warriors." *Newsweek,* October 10, 1983, pp. 38–45.

Brecher, John. "A Secret War for Nicaragua." *Newsweek,* November 8, 1982, pp. 42–53.

Brinkley, Joel. "Covert-Aid Ruling Worries U.S. Aides." *The New York Times,* December 28, 1984, p. A3.

———. "Playing by the Wrong Book on Nicaragua." *The New York Times,* October 21, 1984, p. E5.

———. "C.I.A. Primer Tells Nicaraguan Rebels How to Kill." *The New York Times,* October 17, 1984.

Cannon, Lou, and Don Oberdorfer. "The Mines, the CIA and Shultz's Dissent." *The Washington Post National Weekly Edition,* April 23, 1984, pp. 16–17.

"CIA Said Urging Nicaragua Rebels to Score Gains." *Bridgeport Saturday,* November 26, 1983, p. 26.

Dickey, Christopher, and Edward Cody. "The CIA and It's Not-so-Secret War." *The Washington Post National Weekly Edition,* December 31, 1984, p. 9.

Gelb, Leslie. "Reagan Backing Covert Actions, Officials Assert." *The New York Times,* March 14, 1982, p. 1.

Gerth, Jeff. "Ex-U.S. Intelligence and Military Personnel Supply Anti-Nicaragua Rebels." *The New York Times,* November 8, 1983, p. A12.

Goshko, John, and Joanne Omang. "The Secret War Inside the White House Over Peace With Nicaragua." *The Washington Post National Weekly Edition,* July 23, 1984, p. 16.

Johnson, Haynes. "Reagan's Fixation on Covert Action: He Overlooks Treaty Obligations and a History of Failure." *The Washington Post National Weekly Edition,* November 7, 1983, p. 31.

Kinzer, Stephen. "Nicaragua: The Beleaguered Revolution." *The New York Times Magazine,* August 28, 1983, pp. 22–28.

LeMoyne, James. "The Secret War Boils Over." *Newsweek,* April 11, 1983, pp. 46–50.

Omang, Joanne. "How Will Congress Handle Its Intelligence Role? Ask the CIA." *The Washington Post National Weekly Edition*, December 17, 1984, p. 12.

――――. "Nicaragua: This Is the Big Threat to Our National Security?" *The Washington Post National Weekly Edition*, July 16, 1984, p. 24.

Rositzke, Harry. "It's Time to Get the CIA Out of the Paramilitary Business." *The Washington Post National Weekly Edition*, April 30, 1984, p. 21.

Shapiro, Margaret. "CIA: No Longer a 'Rogue Elephant'?" *The Washington Post National Weekly Edition*, January 14, 1985, p. 12.

Sussman, Barry. "On Central American, Reagan is Consistently Unpersuasive." *The Washington Post National Weekly Edition*, May 14, 1984, p. 37.

Taubman, Philip. "President's Secret War in Nicaragua Backfires." *The New York Times*, April 15, 1984, Section 4. p. 1.

――――. "C.I.A., Too, May Be Hurt in Nicaragua." *The New York Times*, October 16, 1983, p. 1.

――――. "U.S. Officials Say C.I.A. Helped Nicaraguan Rebels Plan Attacks." *The New York Times*, October 16, 1983, p. 1.

"The Illegal U.S. War Against Nicaragua," *Center for Constitutional Rights*, December 1983.

Tolchin, Martin. "Second U.S. Action in Nicaragua Gets Senate Approval." *The New York Times*, November 4, 1983, p. 1.

"U.S. Endorses Covert Aid to Angola Rebels." *The New York Times*, December 15, 1985, p. 2E.

Watson, Russell, et al. "A Furor over the Secret War." *Newsweek*, April 23, 1984, pp. 22–26.

Watson, Russell, and David Martin. "Is Covert Action Necessary?" *Newsweek*, November 8, 1982, pp. 53–55.

Weinraub, Bernard. "Reagan Renews Efforts to Get Arms for Nicaraguan Rebels." *The New York Times*, December 15, 1985, p. 1.

Woodward, Bob, and Charles Babcock. "The CIA's Biggest Covert War Is in Afganistan." *The Washington Post National Weekly Edition*, January 28, 1985, p. 14.

BOOKS

Abernathy, M. Glenn, Dilys M. Hill, and Phil Williams, eds. *The Carter Years: The President and Policy Making*. New York: St. Martin's Press, 1984.

Bailey, Harry A., Jr., ed. *Classics of the American Presidency*. Oak Park, Ill.: Moore Publishing, 1980.

Barber, James David. *The Pulse of Politics: Electing Presidents in the Media Age*. New York: W. W. Norton, 1980.

———, ed. *Race for the Presidency: The Media and the Nominating Process*. Englewood Cliffs, N.J.: Prentice-Hall, 1978.

———. *The Presidential Character: Predicting Performance in the White House*. Englewood Cliffs, N.J.: Prentice-Hall, 1972.

Barger, Harold. *The Impossible Presidency: Illusions and Realities of Executive Power*. Glenview, Ill.: Scott, Foresman, 1984.

Berman, Larry. *The New American Presidency*. Boston: Little, Brown, 1987.

Bessette, Joseph M., and Jeffrey Tulis, eds. *The Presidency in the Constitutional Order*. Baton Rouge: Louisiana State University Press, 1981.

Buchanan, Bruce. *The Presidential Experience: What the Office Does to the Man*. Englewood Cliffs, N.J.: Prentice-Hall, 1978.

Burns, James M. *The Power to Lead: The Crisis of the American Presidency*. New York: Simon and Schuster, 1984.

———. *Presidential Government: The Crucible of Leadership*. Boston: Houghton Mifflin, 1973.

Campbell, John Franklin. *The Foreign Affairs Fudge Factory*. New York: Basic Books, 1971.

Carnoy, Martin, Derek Shearer, and Russell Rumberger. *A New Social Contract: The Economy and Government after Reagan*. New York: Harper and Row, 1983.

Cooper, Chester. *The Last Crusade: America in Vietnam*. New York: Dodd Mead, 1970.

Corwin, Edward S. *The President: Office and Powers*. New York: New York University Press, 1957.

Cronin, Thomas E., ed. *Rethinking the Presidency*. Boston: Little, Brown, 1982.

———. *The State of the Presidency*, 2d ed. Boston: Little, Brown, 1980.

Davis, James W. *The American Presidency: A New Perspective*. New York: Harper and Row, 1987.

Davis, Vincent, ed. *The Post-Imperial Presidency*. New York: Praeger, 1980.

Deakin, James. *Straight Stuff: Reporters, White House and the Truth*. New York: William Morrow, 1984.

DeMause, Lloyd. *Reagan's America*. New York: Creative Roots, 1984.

Dugger, Ronnie. *On Reagan: The Man and His Presidency*. New York: McGraw-Hill, 1983.

Edwards, George C. III. *The Public Presidency: The Pursuit of Popular Support*. New York: St. Martin's Press, 1983.

————. *Presidential Influence in Congress*. San Francisco: W. H. Freeman, 1980.

Edwards, George C. III, and Stephen Wayne, eds. *Studying the Presidency*. Knoxville: University of Tennessee Press, 1983.

Final Senate Watergate Report. New York: Dell Paperback, 1974.

Finer, Herman. *The Presidency: Crisis and Regeneration—An Essay in Possibilities*. Chicago: University of Chicago Press, 1960.

Fishel, Jeff. *Presidents and Promises: From Campaign Pledge to Presidential Performance*. Washington, D.C.: Congressional Quarterly Press, 1985.

Fisher, Louis. *Constitutional Conflicts Between Congress and the Presidency*. Princeton, N.J.: Princeton University Press, 1985.

————. *The Politics of Shared Power: Congress and the Executive*. Washington, D.C.: Congressional Quarterly Press, 1981.

Funderburk, Charles. *Presidents and Politics: The Limits of Power*. Monterey, Calif.: Brooks/Cole Publishing, 1982.

Gartner, Alan, Colin Greer, and Frank Riessman, eds. *Beyond Reagan: Alternatives for the 1980s*. New York: Harper and Row, 1984.

Glad, Betty. *Jimmy Carter: In Search of the Great White House*. New York: W. W. Norton, 1980.

Goldstein, Robert. *Political Repression in Modern America*. New York: Schenkman Publishing, 1978.

Greenberg, Edward. *The Political System: A Radical Approach*, 3d ed. Boston: Little, Brown, 1983.

Greenstein, Fred I., ed. *Leadership in the Modern Presidency*. Cambridge, Mass.: Harvard University Press, 1988.

————. *The Reagan Presidency: An Early Assessment*. Baltimore, Md.: Johns Hopkins University Press, 1983.

Greenstein, Fred I., Larry Berman, and Alvin S. Felzenberg. *Evolution of the Modern Presidency: A Bibliography*. Washington, D.C.: American Enterprise Institute, 1977.

Halberstam, David. *The Best and the Brightest*. Greenwich, Conn.: Fawcett Crest, 1973.

Halperin, Morton, Jerry Berman, Robert Borosage, and Christine Marwick. *The Lawless State: Crimes of the U.S. Intelligence Agencies*. New York: Penguin Books, 1976.

Hargrove, Erwin. *The Power of the Modern Presidency*. New York: Alfred Knopf, 1974.

Hargrove, Erwin C., and Michael Nelson. *President, Politics and Policy*. Baltimore, Md.: Johns Hopkins University Press, 1984.

Hart, Roderick P. *The Sound of Leadership: Presidential Communication in the Modern Age*. Chicago: University of Chicago Press, 1987.

Heclo, Hugh. *Studying the Presidency: Results, Need and Resources*. Naugatuck, Conn.: Ford Foundation, 1977.

Hilsman, Roger. *The Politics of Policy Making in Defense and Foreign Affairs*. New York: Harper and Row, 1971.

Hirschfield, Robert S., ed. *The Power of the Presidency: Concepts and Controversy*, 3d ed. New York: Aldine, 1982.

Hodgson, Godfrey. *All Things to All Men: The False Promise of the Modern American Presidency*. New York: Simon and Schuster, 1980.

Hoopes, Townsend. *The Limits of Intervention*. New York: David McKay, 1970.

Johnson, Loch. *The Making of International Agreements: Congress Confronts the Executive*. New York: New York University Press, 1984.

Kearney, Edward, ed. *Dimensions of the Modern Presidency*. St. Louis: Forum Press, 1981.

Kellerman, Barbara. *The Political Presidency: The Practice of Leadership from Kennedy through Reagan*. New York: Oxford University Press, 1986.

Kelley, Alfred, and Winifred Harbison. *The American Constitution: Its Origins and Development*. New York: W. W. Norton, 1970.

Kessler, Frank. *The Dilemmas of Presidential Leadership: Of Caretakers and Kings*. Englewood Cliffs, N.J.: Prentice-Hall, 1982.

Koenig, Louis. *The Chief Executive*, 5th ed. New York: Harcourt Brace Jovanovich, 1986.

Krukones, Michael G. *Promises and Performance: Presidential Campaigns as Policy Predictors*. Lanham, Md.: University Press of America, 1984.

Laski, Harold. *The American Presidency: An Interpretation*. 1940; reprint ed., New Brunswick, N.J.: Transaction Books, 1980.

Leamer, Laurence. *Make Believe: The Story of Nancy and Ronald Reagan*. New York: Dell, 1983.

Levy, Leonard W. *Jefferson and Civil Liberties: The Darker Side*. Cambridge, Mass.: Harvard University Press, 1963.

Light, Paul C. *Vice Presidential Power: Advice and Influence in the White House*. Baltimore, Md.: Johns Hopkins University Press, 1984.

———. *The President's Agenda: Domestic Policy Choice from Kennedy to Carter*. Baltimore, Md.: Johns Hopkins University Press, 1983.

Longaker, Richard. *The Presidency and Individual Liberties*. Ithaca, N.Y.: Cornell University Press, 1961.

Lovell, John. *Foreign Policy in Perspective: Strategy, Adaptation Decision Making*. New York: Holt, Rinehart and Winston, 1970.

Lowi, Theodore. *The Personal President: Power Invested, Promise Unfulfilled*. Ithaca, N.Y.: Cornell University Press, 1985.

Macy, Christy, and Susan Kaplan. *Documents*. New York: Penguin Books, 1980.

McQuaid, Kim. *Big Business and Presidential Power*. New York: William Morrow, 1982.

Meltsner, Arnold, ed. *Politics and the Oval Office*. San Francisco: Institute for Contemporary Studies, 1981.

Merry, Henry. *The Constitutional Systems*. New York: Praeger, 1986.

Miroff, Bruce. *Pragmatic Illusions*. New York: David McKay, 1976.

Mullen, William F. *Presidential Power and Politics*. New York: St. Martin's Press, 1976.

Muskie, Edmund, Kenneth Rush, and Kenneth Thompson, eds. *The President, the Congress and Foreign Policy*. Lanham, Md.: University Press of America, 1986.

Nelson, Michael, ed. *The Elections of 1984*. Washington, D.C.: Congressional Quarterly Press, 1985.

———. *The Presidency and the Political System*. Washington, D.C.: Congressional Quarterly Press, 1984.

Neustadt, Richard E. *Presidential Power*. New York: John Wiley, 1980.

Orman, John. *Comparing Presidential Behavior: Carter, Reagan and the Macho Presidential Style*. Westport, Conn.: Greenwood Press, 1987.

———. *Presidential Secrecy and Deception: Beyond the Power to Persuade*. Westport, Conn.: Greenwood Press, 1980.

Oudes, Bruce. *From: The President... Richard Nixon's Secret Files*. New York: Harper and Row, 1989.

Page, Benjamin, and Mark Petracca. *The American Presidency*. New York: McGraw-Hill, 1983.

Pessen, Edward. *The Log Cabin Myth: The Social Backgrounds of the Presidents*. New Haven, Conn.: Yale University Press, 1984.

Raskin, Marcus. *The Politics of National Security*. New Brunswick, N.J.: Transaction Books, 1979.

Reagan Ronald. *Where's the Rest of Me*. New York: Karz Publishing, 1981.

Reedy, George. *The Twilight of the Presidency*. New York: New American Library, 1970.

Rockman, Bert. *The Leadership Question: The Presidency and the American System*. New York: Praeger, 1984.

Rogin, Michael Paul. *Ronald Reagan, The Movie, and Other Episodes in Political Demonology*. Berkeley: University of California Press, 1987.

Rossiter, Clinton. *The American Presidency*. New York: Mentor-New American Library, 1960.

Shull, Steven A. *Domestic Policy Formation: Presidential-Congressional Partnership*. Westport, Conn.: Greenwood Press, 1983.

Sickels, Robert. *The Presidency: An Introduction*. Englewood Cliffs, N.J.: Prentice-Hall, 1980.

Smith, Hedrick. *The Power Game*. New York: Random House, 1988.

Sorensen, Theodore. *A Different Kind of Presidency*. New York: Harper and Row, 1984.

Speakes, Larry. *Speaking Out: Inside the Reagan White House*. New York: Scribner's 1988.

Spitzer, Robert. *The Presidency and Public Policy*. Tuscaloosa: University of Alabama Press, 1983.

Steinfield, Melvin. *Our Racist Presidents: From Washington to Nixon*. San Ramon, Calif.: Consensus Publishers, 1972.

Talbott, Strobe. *The Russians and Reagan*. New York: Vintage Books, 1984.

Tebbel, John, and Sarah Miles Watts. *The Press and the Presidency*. New York: Oxford University Press, 1985.

Thompson, Kenneth, ed. *The White House Press on the Presidency*. Lanham, Md.: University Press of America, 1983.

U.S. Congress, Senate. Final Report of the Select Committee to Study Governmental Operations with Respect to Intelligence Activities (*Church Committee Reports*). Washington, D.C.: U.S. Government Printing Office, 1976.

Van der Linden, Frank. *The Real Reagan*. New York: William Morrow and Co., 1981.

The White House Transcripts. New York: New York Times, Bantam Books, 1974.

White, Theodore. *America in Search of Itself: The Making of the Presidents, 1956–1980*. New York: Harper and Row, 1982.

Wills, Garry. *Reagan's America*. New York: Doubleday, 1987.

Wise, David. *The American Police State*. New York: Random House, 1976.

Wise, David. *The Politics of Lying*. New York Random House, 1973.

JOURNALS

Ahrari, Mohammed. "Contemporary Constraints on Presidential Leadership," *Presidential Studies Quarterly* 11, no. 2 (Spring 1981): 233–243.

Arnhart, Larry. "The God-Like Prince: John Locke, Executive Prerogative and the American Presidency," *Presidential Studies Quarterly* 9, no. 2 (Spring, 1979): 121–130.

Bailey, Christopher. "President Reagan, the U.S. Senate and American Foreign Policy, 1981–1986," *Journal of American Studies* 21 (August 1987): 167–181.

Barilleaux, Ryan. "Post Modern American Presidency," *Presidency Research* 10, no. 1 (Winter 1987): 15–18.

Citrin, Jack, and Donald Philip Green. "Presidential Leadership and the Resurgence of Trust in Government," *British Journal of Political Science* 16 (October 1986): 431–453.

Cronin, Thomas E. "A Conversation-Interview on the American Presidency with Louis W. Koenig," *Presidential Studies Quarterly* 16 (Fall 1986): 761–771.

———. "On the American Presidency: A Conversation with James MacGregor Burns," *Presidential Studies Quarterly* 16 (Summer 1986): 528–542.

Edwards, George C., III. "The Two Presidencies: A Reevaluation," *American Politics Quarterly* 14 (July 1986): 247–263.

Genovese, Michael. "The Return of the Imperial Presidency," *Presidency Research* 9, no. 1 (Fall, 1986): 28–29.

———. "Presidential Leadership and Crisis Management," *Presidential Studies Quarterly* 16 (Spring 1986): 300–309.

Henkin, Louis. "Foreign Affairs and the Constitution," *Foreign Affairs* 67 (Winter 1987/88): 284–310.

Holt, Carol Lynn. "Executive Privilege," *Presidential Studies Quarterly* 16 (Spring 1986): 237–246.

Jameson, Donald. "The 'Iran Affair,' Presidential Authority and Covert Operations," *Strategic Review* 15 (Winter 1987): 24–30.

Ladd, Everett C. "The Foreign Policy Record: Reagan's Sphere of Influence," *Public Opinion* 8 (Summer 1986): 3–6.

Levey, Jules. "Richard Nixon as Elder Statesman," *Journal of Psycho-History* 14 (Spring 1986): 427–448.

Lowi, Theodore. "Presidential Power: Restoring the Balance," *Political Science Quarterly* 100, no. 2 (Summer 1985): 185–213.

Mansfield, Harvey, Jr. "The Modern Doctrine of Executive Power," *Presidential Studies Quarterly* 17 (Spring 1987): 237–252.

Miroff, Bruce. "Presidential Leverage over Social Movements: The Johnson White House and Civil Rights," *Journal of Politics* 43, no. 1 (February 1981): 2–22.

Morris, Bernard. "Presidential Accountability in Foreign Policy," *Congress and the Presidency* 15 (Autumn 1986): 157–176.

Rockman, Bert. "Studying the American Presidency in the Bicentennial Year," *Presidency Research* 10, no. 1 (Fall 1987): 11–13.

———. "The Modern Presidency and Theories of Accountability: Old Wine and Old Bottles." *Congress and the Presidency* 15 (Autumn 1986): 135–156.

Rose, Richard. "The Post-Modern Presidency: The World Closes in on the White House," *Presidency Research* 10, no. 2 (Spring 1988): 5–8.

Rubner, Michael. "The Reagan Administration, the 1973 War Powers Resolution and the Invasion of Grenada," *Political Science Quarterly* 100, no 4 (Winter 1985–86): 627–647.

Small, Melvin. "Influencing the Decision Makers: The Vietnam Experience." *Journal of Peace Research* 24 (June 1987): 185–198.

Taylor, Maxwell. "The Legitimate Claims of National Security," *Foreign Affairs* 52, no. 3 (April 1974): 577–594.

Timbers, Edwin. "The Supreme Court and the President as Commander in Chief," *Presidential Studies Quarterly* 16, no. 2 (Spring 1986): 224–236.

Vaughn, Stephen. "Spies, National Security, and the 'Inertia Projector': The Secret Service Films of Ronald Reagan," *American Quarterly* 39 (Fall 1987) 355–380.

Wolfers, Arnold. "National Security as an Ambiguous Symbol," *Political Science Quarterly* 67, no. 4 (December 1952).

MISCELLANEOUS

Boyan, Stephen. "Prerogative, the Constitution and the Presidency After Watergate." Paper presented at the annual meeting of the American Political Science Association, Chicago, September 2–5, 1976.

Deakin, James. "The Imperial President and the Imperial Media," in *The American Presidency, Principle and Problems*, vol. 2, ed. Kenneth Thompson. New York: University Press of America, 1983.

Franklin, Daniel. "Presidential Prerogative and the Legislative Veto." Paper presented annual meeting of the American Political Science Association, Chicago, September 3–6, 1987.

Koenig, Louis. "Reassessing the Imperial Presidency," in *The Power to Govern: Proceedings of the Academy of Political Science*, ed. Richard Pious, 34, no. 2 (1981): 31–44.

Ridgeway, James. "Home Is Where the Covert Action Is: Harassment of Peace Groups Raises Questions," *The Village Voice*, December 16, 1986.

Schieffer, Bob, and Gary Paul Gates. "That Bush-Rather Blowup: A New Twist," *TV Guide*, July 8–14, 1989, pp. 33–36.

Thomas, Norman C. "The Presidency and Critical Scholarship in Perspective," Paper presented at the annual meeting of the American Political Science Association, Chicago, September 3–6, 1987.

——. "Recent Developments and Accountability: Presidential Accountability Since Watergate," Paper presented at the annual meeting of the Midwest Political Science Association, Chicago, April 20–22, 1978.

Wright, Michael, and Caroline R. Herron. "Another Day in the Oval Office," *The New York Times*, February 27, 1981, p. 2E.

Index

About the Author

JOHN ORMAN is a professor in the Political Science Department at Fairfield University. He is the author of *Comparing Presidential Behavior* (Greenwood Press, 1987), *Presidential Secrecy and Deception* (Greenwood Press, 1980), and *The Politics of Rock Music*.